# Contrastive Reasons

# Contrastive Reasons

Justin Snedegar

**UNIVERSITY PRESS**

Great Clarendon Street, Oxford, OX2 6DP,
United Kingdom

Oxford University Press is a department of the University of Oxford.
It furthers the University's objective of excellence in research, scholarship,
and education by publishing worldwide. Oxford is a registered trade mark of
Oxford University Press in the UK and in certain other countries

© Justin Snedegar 2017

The moral rights of the author have been asserted

First Edition published in 2017

Impression: 1

All rights reserved. No part of this publication may be reproduced, stored in
a retrieval system, or transmitted, in any form or by any means, without the
prior permission in writing of Oxford University Press, or as expressly permitted
by law, by licence or under terms agreed with the appropriate reprographics
rights organization. Enquiries concerning reproduction outside the scope of the
above should be sent to the Rights Department, Oxford University Press, at the
address above

You must not circulate this work in any other form
and you must impose this same condition on any acquirer

Published in the United States of America by Oxford University Press
198 Madison Avenue, New York, NY 10016, United States of America

British Library Cataloguing in Publication Data
Data available

Library of Congress Control Number: 2016955211

ISBN 978-0-19-878593-4

Printed in Great Britain by
Clays Ltd, St Ives plc

Links to third party websites are provided by Oxford in good faith and
for information only. Oxford disclaims any responsibility for the materials
contained in any third party website referenced in this work.

*To Emmy, for love and support*
*And to my parents, for always being proud of me*

# Contents

*Acknowledgments* ix
*Preface* xiii

1 Contrastivism and Reasons 1
   1.1 Reasons and Contrastivism 2
   1.2 Reasons and the Contrastivist Program 8
   1.3 The Plan 21

2 Reason Claims 24
   2.1 A Simple Argument 24
   2.2 A Stronger Argument 28
   2.3 Contrastivism 32
   2.4 Other 'Rather than' Ascriptions 36
   2.5 Negative Reason Existentials 38
   2.6 Looking Forward 44

3 Favoring 45
   3.1 Why Resist Contrastivism? 45
   3.2 Shallow Contrastivism 46
   3.3 Favoring 51
   3.4 Contrastive Reasons and Favoring 58
   3.5 Looking Forward 62

4 Promotion 63
   4.1 The Need for Constraints 64
   4.2 Promotion 68
   4.3 Contrastive Reasons and Promotion 76
   4.4 Contrastive Reasons as Better Reasons? 81
   4.5 Providing the Constraints 82
   4.6 Non-Promotional Reasons 87
   4.7 Where we Are 89

5 Intransitivity 91
   5.1 Transitivity and Reasons 92
   5.2 Intransitivity 95
   5.3 Intransitivity and Contrastivism 101
   5.4 Contrast-Sensitive Importance 103
   5.5 Remaining Questions 109
   5.6 Conclusion 113

6 Withholding 114
   6.1 Withholding Belief and Contrastive Reasons 115
   6.2 Withholding Intention 129
   6.3 Wrap Up 137

*References* 139
*Index* 147

# Acknowledgments

This book began to take shape, as my dissertation, during the summer of 2011. But work towards it really began during my second year of graduate school at the University of Southern California in 2009. I spent that year working with Mark Schroeder, who would eventually become my dissertation supervisor, developing a contrastive view of deontic modals like 'ought' and 'must'. That eventually expanded into the work on reasons in this book. I also spent a lot of time talking to Steve Finlay about these issues during this time. So Mark and Steve have been involved from the earliest stages of this project.

Thanks to Steve for always being very encouraging, and for, at the same time, offering sharp criticisms. A common experience was getting a set of comments, which began with something like 'This is great! I think this is all basically right', followed by pages of very serious criticisms. I find myself agreeing with Steve frequently, especially about metaethics; it was great, as a graduate student, having someone around who shared my philosophical instincts. Jake Ross has also been involved from early on. It was Jake who suggested that I focus on reasons, and expressed some sympathy for contrastivism, which was very encouraging to me.

Many of the other faculty members at USC were very helpful at various stages of the project; I will mention just a few in particular. Scott Soames talked with me about this material several times, and, more importantly, did more than anyone during my first couple of years as a graduate student to teach me how to do philosophy well. Ralph Wedgwood arrived after I was well into the project, but showed a lot of enthusiasm for my work and provided very useful feedback. Thanks are also due to Barry Schein, both for teaching me most of what I know about formal semantics and for serving as the outside member of my dissertation committee—something he has done for many, many philosophy students, to the great benefit of USC philosophy!

Thanks to all of my fellow graduate students for contributing to the great community. For especially helpful discussions about this work, thanks to Indrek Reiland, Julia Staffel, Josh Crabill, Alida Liberman, Lewis Powell, Johannes Schmitt, and Sam Shpall. Thanks also to Jason Raibley, who wasn't a USC graduate student, but has been a great friend and philosophical interlocutor since my time in California. I've learned a lot about normativity and rigorous thinking about ethics from talking with Shyam Nair. Justin Dallmann helped me with several parts of this book, especially with some of the central parts of Chapter 4. Thanks to him, and to Amanda Dallmann, for feeding Emmy and me many Friday nights and for being wonderful friends. Finally, thanks to Ben Lennertz. He's helped me in one way or another with most of the work in this book, and talked with me about philosophy, fantasy baseball, and life (in that order, more or less) constantly over the last eight years.

Outside of USC, two people were, and continue to be, especially encouraging and helpful. Fabrizio Cariani has given me great feedback on much of my work, including big chunks of material from this book. Walter Sinnott-Armstrong has been more consistently enthusiastic about this material than anyone, including me. He has given me very insightful comments on the entire book, and arranged for me to spend a couple of weeks at Duke University in the fall of 2013, talking about the manuscript with some of his graduate students; thanks also to those students. Besides Mark and Steve, Walter has probably had the biggest influence on the book.

Thanks are also due to the philosophy department at West Virginia University. Everyone in the department was wonderful, but thanks especially to Sharon Ryan and Andrew Cullison (who was at WVU while I was an undergraduate there). They taught me how to do philosophy and encouraged me to pursue it. Andy was the first person who made me even consider the possibility of being a philosopher for a living. Besides being an academic mentor, Sharon also made sure there was money available from the department to help me pay for conferences, summer seminars, and graduate school applications.

The philosophy department at the University of St Andrews has been the perfect environment to polish this work and to settle into my career. Thanks to my colleagues and students for that, and in particular for feedback on this material.

Thanks to John Brunero and Hille Paakkunainen, who read this book for Oxford University Press, and provided pages and pages of wonderful comments, questions, and criticisms.

My greatest professional debt is to Mark Schroeder. He bought into the fruitfulness of the project—even if he didn't buy contrastivism!—from the start, and his dedication to it was crucial in helping me see it through.

ACKNOWLEDGMENTS xi

Mark has influenced the work here immensely; this will be obvious from the beginning. His own work has served as part of my toolkit, as a target, and as an inspiration. The ideas here are mine, but I wouldn't have had most of them if Mark hadn't dragged them out of me. I can't imagine a better or more invested advisor; thanks, Mark.

Thanks to my parents for supporting me, encouraging me, and being proud of me—even though philosophy took me first 2,500 miles away to Los Angeles, and then 3,600 miles away in the other direction, to St Andrews. My dad has made sure that mine is probably some of the most well-known work in metaethics among bikers from south-eastern West Virginia. My debt to my mom is simply immeasurable; she made some very serious sacrifices to make sure that my sisters and I would be successful, and I can't thank her enough for that.

Finally, thanks most of all to my best friend, sounding board, gourmet chef, and wife, Emmy. She has been the best possible partner. Throughout our five years in Los Angeles and the last three and a half in Scotland, she has been unwaveringly supportive and loving. Without her, this book wouldn't exist; lots of more important things would also be missing.

Previous versions of some of the material from this book have been published elsewhere. The bulk of the material from Chapter 2 appears in two articles: 'Reason Claims and Contrastivism about Reasons', in *Philosophical Studies*, 166/2 (2013), 231–42, and 'Negative Reason Existentials', in *Thought*, 2 (2013), 108–16. An earlier version of Chapter 4 is published as 'Contrastive Reasons and Promotion', in *Ethics*, 125/1 (2014), 39–63. Thanks to these journals for permission to use this material here.

# Preface

This book develops and defends a contrastive view of normative reasons, according to which they are fundamentally reasons for one thing rather than another, or for one thing out of some range of alternatives. Reasons for something relative to one set of alternatives may not be reasons for that same thing relative to some other alternatives. This is in opposition to nearly all existing work on reasons, which assumes without argument—even without mention—that reasons are reasons for actions *simpliciter*, independently of what we're comparing the action to.

I argue that this contrastive view is supported by (i) our *talk* about reasons, (ii) the idea that reasons *favor* the things they are reasons for, and (iii) the idea that reasons involve the *promotion* of things such as desires, goals, or values. These arguments build, step by step, to a detailed version of contrastivism that can both claim advantages over the traditional non-contrastive picture and avoid problems that face less well-developed versions of contrastivism.

One thread running through the book is an exploration of the *depth* of contrastivism. Chapter 2 argues that contrastivism goes at least as deep as our use of the word 'reason'—this word (as used to ascribe normative reasons) should be given a contrastive treatment. Chapter 3 argues that contrastivism actually goes deeper, to the normative reason, or favoring, relation that normative philosophers are concerned with. Chapter 4, though, argues for a somewhat moderate contrastive theory. The normative reason relation is indeed contrastive, but we need not—in fact, we'd better not—adopt the deepest possible form of contrastivism.

Given the central place of reasons in normative philosophy, we should expect that contrastivism will have upshots throughout areas such as ethics, practical rationality, and epistemology. In the final two chapters of this book, I start to explore this idea. This is just a start, but it suggests that exploring further applications for contrastivism is likely to be a fruitful area for future research.

# 1

# Contrastivism and Reasons

For a few wonderful years, I lived in Thai Town in Los Angeles. I was surrounded by delicious, cheap Thai food. Fortunately, I was often in the mood for just that. Two of my favorites were Jitlada and Red Corner Asia. So imagine I'm trying to decide where to go for dinner, and am craving Thai food. Is this a reason for me to go to Jitlada? It may seem clear that it is, since they serve delicious Thai food there. But there are many other places around, including Red Corner Asia, that serve delicious Thai food. Suppose in addition that Jitlada is often very crowded, and that there's a chance that, if I go there, I won't be able to get a table. On the other hand, Red Corner Asia always has free tables. In this case, it seems clear that the fact that I'm in the mood for Thai food isn't a reason to go to Jitlada *rather than* go to Red Corner Asia. On the other hand, the fact that I'm in the mood for Thai food certainly is a reason to go to Jitlada rather than go to Paru's Indian restaurant, where they don't serve Thai food.

This is a special case of a very general observation: often some consideration is a reason to perform an action rather than some alternatives, but not a reason to perform it rather than some other alternatives.[1] A theory of reasons needs to explain this.

In this book, I defend a theory of reasons that takes this observation seriously. On this theory, called *contrastivism* about reasons, reasons are always reasons for one thing rather than another, or more generally reasons for one thing out of a certain set of alternatives, instead of reasons for things *simpliciter*, as has been traditionally assumed. So to know whether *r* is a reason to *A*, we have to know 'rather than what?'. Obviously nothing I've said yet establishes that this theory is true. Establishing that is the goal of this book. To do so, I'll develop a detailed version of contrastivism,

---

[1] See Ross (2006: ch. 9) and Sinnott-Armstrong (2006: ch. 5) for this observation.

motivating each step along the way by arguing that contrastivism gives us the best way to make sense of important and puzzling features of reasons. Since reasons are so important in philosophy—talk about reasons shows up in any field in which *normativity* plays an important role—this book will include discussion from several fields, including ethics, practical reasoning, and epistemology.

## 1.1 Reasons and Contrastivism

This book advocates contrastivism about reasons. To get clear on just what this view is, we need to get clear on two things: reasons and contrastivism.

### 1.1.1 Reasons

The theory I will develop here concerns *normative* reasons. These are considerations, usually taken to be facts or true propositions, that count in favor of or against doing various things: performing actions, believing propositions, and having a variety of other attitudes.[2] For example, the fact that I'm in the mood for Thai food is a reason for me to go to Red Corner Asia, and the fact that you are sleeping in the next room is a reason against turning the volume on my stereo up high. These reasons are what are often called *pro tanto*: they count in favor of or against performing various actions (or having various attitudes) with a certain strength or weight. There may be some reasons for me to go to Red Corner Asia— I am in the mood for Thai food, it is nearby, and so on—and some reasons against doing so—it is crowded at this time of day, it is expensive, and so on. These *pro tanto* reasons for and against the action contribute, in some way, to what I ought to do.[3] Reasons for an action may outweigh the reasons against it, or vice versa; similarly, the reasons for one action may outweigh the reasons for another action. Thus, contrastivism is not a thesis, at least not primarily, about what there is *most reason* to do, overall, or what there is *decisive* reason to do. It is rather a thesis about these *pro tanto* reasons, that contribute to what there is reason to do, overall.

---

[2] This talk of 'counting in favor' is ubiquitous, but see especially Scanlon (1998). Hieronymi (2005) thinks that thinking of reasons primarily in these terms leads to problems, though even she agrees that reasons do count in favor of the things they are reasons for.

[3] Broome (2004), for example, uses the term *pro tanto*; Dancy (2004), on the other hand, uses 'contributory' to talk about the same kinds of reasons.

Normative reasons are distinct from two other sorts of reasons. First, they are distinct from *motivating* reasons—the reasons for which agents do the things they do. These are cited in explanations of the actions of agents. Of course, it is plausible that the facts which are an agent's motivating reasons could also be normative reasons for that agent. But the motivating and normative reason relations are distinct. Second, normative reasons are distinct from *explanatory* reasons, which we cite in explaining phenomena more generally (plausibly, motivating reasons are a species of explanatory reasons). For example, the reason why the faucet is leaking is that it needs a new washer. Motivating reasons and explanatory reasons more generally do not count in favor of or against doing anything; they are rather explanations why things happen. Besides a short discussion of explanation near the end of this chapter, I will not have much more to say about these kinds of reasons; thus, when I talk about reasons, I will usually not include the qualifier 'normative'.[4]

## 1.1.2 Contrastivism

I will be almost exclusively concerned with contrastivism about reasons. But writers have proposed contrastive theories of several important philosophical concepts. Contrastivism about explanation, for example, goes back at least to van Fraassen (1980).[5] Staying in the philosophy of science, philosophers have more recently offered contrastive theories of confirmation.[6] The basic idea is that some fact $e$ explains some other fact $p$ rather than another fact $q$, or confirms some hypothesis $h$ rather than some other hypothesis $j$, instead of explaining $p$ or confirming $h$ *simpliciter*. More recently, contrastive theories of knowledge—the view that knowledge is always knowledge of $p$ rather than $q$—have become popular.[7] Blaauw (2012) has argued that knowledge is contrastive because belief is contrastive. Sinnott-Armstrong (2004, 2006, 2008) has argued instead that knowledge is contrastive because justification is contrastive. In metaphysics, Schaffer (2005a, 2012) has argued that causation is contrastive.

---

[4] For more thorough discussion of these and other distinctions, see the opening chapters of many books about reasons, including Darwall (1983), Dancy (2000), Schroeder (2007), Alvarez (2010).
[5] See also Garfinkel (1981), Lipton (1990), Hitchcock (1996).
[6] Chandler (2007, 2013). See Fitelson (2012) for critical discussion.
[7] See Morton and Karjalainen (2003), Schaffer (2004, 2005b, 2007, 2008). A predecessor is Dretske (1970).

And, perhaps most importantly for my purposes, several writers have proposed contrastive theories of 'ought'.[8] In the most general terms, contrastivism about some property or relation $R$ is the view that $R$ includes an argument place that must be filled by a set of alternatives. So $R$ holds or fails to hold only of some number of things relative to sets of alternatives.

Contrastivism about some concept is often motivated by showing how judgments involving the concept appear to be *question-relative*, so that the truth value of a claim involving the concept can vary depending on a relevant question. For example, Schaffer (2007) has argued that to know that $p$ is to know that $p$ as the answer to a particular question, salient in the context. Thus, knowing that $p$ when the salient question is $Q$ does not guarantee that you know that $p$ when the salient question is $Q'$. And Cariani (2013) describes his contrastive view of 'ought' as the view that 'ought' is relative to a deliberative question: the question of what to do. The move from question-relativity to contrastivism is a natural one, because a standard view of questions in formal semantics treats them as partitions on (some subspace of) logical space, or as a set of alternatives with each alternative corresponding to one cell of the partition.[9] So, on this view, question-relativity just is alternative-relativity.

There's a question about how to implement this idea: how do we determine the relevant set of alternatives for evaluating whether some consideration is a reason, whether an agent knows a proposition, and so on? Sometimes it's provided explicitly. Most obviously, the alternatives can be provided explicitly using a 'rather than' clause, as in 'There's a reason to go to Red Corner Asia rather than Paru's'. Here the alternatives are clearly going to Red Corner Asia and going to Paru's. Since these kinds of ascriptions make the alternative very obvious, I'll appeal to them frequently. Similarly, some writers have argued that knowledge-*wh* ascriptions, such as 'I know when to hold 'em' and 'I know what you did last summer', relate an agent and a question, where the *wh*-clause provides the question explicitly ('When to hold 'em?', 'What did you do last summer?').[10] Of course, even if we are given the question, we need

---

[8] See Sloman (1970), Jackson (1985), Finlay (2009, 2014), Cariani (2009, 2013), Kierland (2012), Snedegar (2012), Finlay and Snedegar (2014).

[9] See Hamblin (1958), Higginbotham (1993, 1996), Groenendijk and Stokhof (1997) for this sort of view of questions.

[10] See Schaffer (2007), Stanley (2011). Ascriptions that explicitly include a question are very natural for knowledge and explanation ascriptions, but not for reason, 'ought', or causal ascriptions.

to know the possible answers: which ones count as relevant, and how are we to individuate answers? Moreover, many ascriptions do not explicitly introduce—or even let on that there are—alternatives, as in 'You know that I love you' and 'The fact that I love you is a reason for you to love me back'. What are the sets of alternatives relative to which we should interpret these sorts of claims?

The most natural view is a version of *contextualism*, according to which the argument place is filled by some contextually relevant set of alternatives. There are various ways to make a set of alternatives relevant. For example, using intonational stress, as in 'There's a reason to *drive* to the store' (letting italics mark stress), makes relevant a set of alternatives in which the alternatives differ in (the object corresponding to) the stressed item, for example, {drive to the store, bike to the store, walk to the store}. If I say instead, 'There's a reason to drive to the *store*', the relevant alternatives might be {drive to the store, drive to church, drive to campus}.[11] Other features of the context can make an alternative salient, as well. For example, Schaffer (2007), Finlay (2009), Cariani (2013), and Finlay and Snedegar (2014) all appeal to questions under discussion.[12] If I'm deliberating between going to Red Corner Asia, going to Jitlada, and going to Paru's, the natural set of alternatives relative to which an ascription like 'The fact that my guest loves Indian food is a reason to go to Paru's' is to be evaluated is {go to Red Corner Asia, go to Jitlada, go to Paru's}. Thus, on this simple contextualist view, the speaker's intentions will play a large part in determining the set of alternatives relative to which we should evaluate reason ascriptions.[13]

However we choose to develop it, the central contrastivist (about reasons) semantic claim is that reason claims must be interpreted and evaluated relative to some set of alternatives or other. The central metaphysical claim is that the reason relation includes a place for a set of alternatives in addition to the more standard places for facts (or considerations), agents, and actions (and perhaps other relata, like times). Moreover,

---

[11] See Dretske (1970), Rooth (1992), Schaffer (2005b, 2007, 2008).

[12] See Roberts (2012) for compelling arguments that we need the notion of a question under discussion in our theory of communication, independently of contrastivism.

[13] I don't think this speaker–contextualist version is necessary. For example, we might have a view on which the set of alternatives is provided by the context of assessment, or perhaps even by the relevant agent's (not necessarily the speaker, and not necessarily in the speaker's context) circumstances, if we develop things in the right way. But I'll develop the contextualist version of the view.

contrastivism is the view that, holding fixed these other relata, we can still get variations in whether some fact is a reason for an action by varying the sets of alternatives. I will have more to say about this in the next chapter when I develop a contrastive account of reason ascriptions.

There are two interesting features of these sets of alternatives. First, they are not necessarily exhaustive of logical space, or of all of the things that it's possible for the agent to do.[14] Some alternatives are left out, for one reason or another (for example, they are irrelevant).[15] Second, the options are divided up at a more or less fine-grained level of detail. For example, one particularly coarse-grained set would be something like {go to Red Corner Asia, don't go to Red Corner Asia}, while a more fine-grained one would be {go to Red Corner Asia, go to Spicy BBQ, go to Paru's}. This is what Yalcin (2011) and, following him, Cariani (2013) call *resolution sensitivity*. The idea is that we partition logical space at higher or lower resolutions; alternatives that are distinct at a higher resolution may be blurred together at a lower resolution. Either or both of these features can be exploited to solve various puzzles.[16] I'll end up making use of both of these features in my version of contrastivism about reasons.

Given the standard treatment of questions I mentioned earlier, originally due to Hamblin (1958), it's easy to see how both of these features could come along with question-relativity. Non-exhaustivity comes along

---

[14] It's not quite right to talk about questions or alternatives partitioning (part of) logical space if you treat the elements of the set as actions, as I've been doing, rather than as propositions. So, if we take this idea of question-relativity seriously, there are two options. First, we can say that, strictly speaking, reasons are reasons for propositions (i.e. a reason for the proposition that you A) rather than for actions (i.e. a reason for you to A). (cf. Finlay 2006, 2014.) Second, we can say that reasons really are reasons for actions, but, in our model, hold the agent fixed so that we can treat actions as propositions (i.e. the set of worlds in which the relevant agent performs the relevant action). See Cariani (2013) for discussion of this last strategy.

[15] Compare the relevant alternatives theory of knowledge in Lewis (1996), Dretske (1970).

[16] (Skorupski, 2010: 38) explicitly endorses a view of reasons for action on which they are relativized to what he calls 'choice sets': "When we think of think of sufficient reasons for doing something [...] we assume some exhaustive partitioning of actions, within which one and only one action must be done. Call an exhaustive partitioning of actions a choice set; 'inaction' and likewise the action of further deliberation are members of this set." Skorupski's view does not count as a contrastivist view as I've defined it above, because he does not accept non-exhaustivity. But he does accept resolution sensitivity, so, as far as that goes, I'm sympathetic. But, since I think we need to adopt non-exhaustivity to gain lots of the advantages of contrastivism, I reject Skorupski's view.

because questions need not partition the entirety of logical space—sometimes they partition only a subspace. This can happen, for example, when the question has presuppositions: possibilities in which those presuppositions fail are not in the subspace partitioned by the question. Resolution sensitivity comes along simply because the question has to partition this subspace at some resolution or other. Which possibilities are left out as irrelevant and the resolution at which the relevant possibilities are partitioned will both depend, among other things, on context (on the contextualist version of contrastivism). They may also be determined explicitly by *wh*-complements (in the case of 'knows', for example) or by 'rather than' clauses.

So contrastivism about reasons is the thesis that reasons to $A$ are always reasons to $A$ relative to, or out of, some particular set of alternatives. The set of alternatives need not be exhaustive of all of the things the agent could possibly do, and the alternatives in the set must be divided up at some particular level of detail, or resolution. This view fits naturally with a realistic picture of deliberation, which, I'll assume, involves at least in part consideration of one's reasons for action. First, when we deliberate about what to do, we don't always do so over every possible alternative. Second, we can consider the options only at some level of detail or other. The contrastivist holds that as the relevant possibilities, or the resolution at which they are individuated, varies, the reasons can vary. Which set of alternatives is relevant can vary depending on features of the context. This set must be supplied before we can say whether $r$ is a reason to $A$ or not, since it can be or fail to be a reason only relative to a set of alternatives. Arguments for contrastivism claim that, as the set of alternatives shifts, the reasons for and against a given action can vary—what was a reason to $A$ relative to one set may not be a reason to $A$ relative to a different set.

It may be helpful to compare the contrastivist thesis, that whether some consideration is a reason for an action or attitude depends on what we are comparing that action or attitude to, with a more widely accepted thesis. This is the thesis that whether a consideration is a reason for an action or attitude depends on the circumstances, which may include the *available* alternatives. For example, if saving Sue plus some other people is an available alternative, there may be reasons against saving *only* Sue that would not exist if saving Sue plus some other people were not an available alternative. Contrastivism is compatible with this view, and indeed with the view that reasons can depend on many other features of the choice situation.[17] But the central contrastivist thesis is that, even once we fix all of these features, the reasons may vary depending on the specific comparisons. By way of illustration, in the opening example, even if we assume that all three of Jitlada, Red Corner Asia, and Paru's Indian restaurant are available options, and hold all other features of the circumstance fixed, whether the fact that I'm in the mood for Thai food is a reason to go to Jitlada will depend on the comparison. It is a reason to go to Jitlada rather than go to Paru's, but it is not a reason to go to Jitlada rather than go to Red Corner Asia.

We might make the circumstances more fine-grained by building the relevant alternatives (including their resolution), or the particular comparison we are making, into our conception of a context or choice situation. I have no objection to this. In that case, the kind of relativity in reasons that contrastivism posits would just be another kind of context- or circumstance-relativity. Nevertheless, it is not a kind of relativity that has been much explored.

## 1.2 Reasons and the Contrastivist Program

I have just been discussing contrastivism as a general philosophical program that has been applied to several important concepts such as knowledge, justification, 'ought', and explanation. One thing to notice is that all (or at least almost all) of the concepts for which contrastivism seems plausible and fruitful are intimately related to reasons, of some kind or other. So a tempting thought is that contrastivism about reasons is really central, and underwrites contrastivism about all of these other concepts. In fact, Walter Sinnott-Armstrong has exactly this thought:

> In my view, epistemologists need contrasts in their analyses of knowledge and justified belief because knowledge and justified belief require reasons [...] and reasons are always reasons for one thing as opposed to another. [...] The same rationale will then apply to any other kind of reasons, and many philosophical issues concern reasons. Epistemologists study reasons *for belief*. Moral philosophers investigate moral reasons *for action*. Aestheticians explore reasons *to like* or *to value* certain art, music, and so on. Philosophers of science analyze

---

[17] Jonathan Dancy's work on *holism* about reasons is a particularly clear example of this kind of thesis (see, e.g., Dancy, 2004), but I believe it is widely held.

explanations, which give reasons *why* events happen. And so on. Because reasons are central to all these areas of philosophy, and all reasons are relative to contrasts, all these areas of philosophy can benefit from introducing a new place for contrasts into the relations used in analyses.[18]

This suggests a kind of argument to the best explanation: the best explanation for why these other concepts—justification, obligation, explanation, and so on—are contrastive is that they inherit it from the contrastivity of reasons.

While I agree both that reasons are contrastive and that this is a tempting thought, I do not think this is ultimately a very compelling argument for contrastivism about reasons. To show why, I will call into question both the necessity and the sufficiency of contrastivism about normative reasons for contrastivism about the normative notions of justification and 'ought'. Of course, since this is just an argument to the best explanation, this does not show that it cannot work. But the arguments will involve the introduction of plausible views that accept contrastivism about reasons without accepting contrastivism about the other normative concept ('ought' or justification), or vice versa. All of this should make us suspicious of the inference Sinnott-Armstrong draws.

I will also consider the relationship between normative reasons and explanation to see whether adopting a contrastive view of explanation puts pressure on us to adopt contrastivism about normative reasons. I'll suggest that, at the very least, the argument from contrastivism about explanation to contrastivism about reasons requires some controversial assumptions.

I want to emphasize that, even if Sinnott-Armstrong is correct that contrastivism about reasons would be the best explanation for contrastivism about all of these other concepts, for the argument actually to support contrastivism about reasons, we would first have to accept contrastivism about all of the other concepts. So Sinnott-Armstrong's argument, regardless of its merits *given* the assumption that these other concepts are contrastive, is at the very least more *indirect* than we might hope for. So the goal of this discussion, in the context of this book, is to motivate looking for more direct evidence that reasons are contrastive.

---

[18] Sinnott-Armstrong (2008: 257–8).

## 1.2.1 Reasons and justification

Contrastivism about justification is the view that you can be justified in believing that *p* only out of, or relative to, a certain set of alternatives *Q*. Contrastivism about justification leads naturally to contrastivism about knowledge, since knowledge requires justification, and contrastivism about knowledge has become a major player in the epistemological literature. Nevertheless, I'm going to focus on contrastivism about justification here, since justification is more directly tied to reasons (the relationship between knowledge and reasons is plausibly mediated by justification).

One motivation for adopting contrastivism about justification is that it seems to offer a solution to the infamous closure paradox. It seems that Moore is justified in believing that he has hands. And he's justified in believing that, if he has hands, then he's not a handless brain-in-a-vat. But it also seems that he's not justified in believing that he's not a handless brain-in-a-vat. The contrastivist can say that Moore is justified in believing that he has hands rather than, say, flippers. But he's not justified in believing that he's not a handless brain-in-a-vat rather than that he has hands. In other words, he's justified in believing that he has hands out of some sets of alternatives, but not out of others. In this section, I'm just going to assume for the sake of discussion that justification is contrastive. So now what we need to do to establish contrastivism about reasons, along the lines suggested by Sinnott-Armstrong, is (i) show how justification is related to reasons, and (ii) show how this relationship puts pressure on us to accept contrastivism about reasons if we accept contrastivism about justification.

So what is the relationship between justification and reasons? A very intuitive first answer is that you can be justified in believing a proposition only if you have sufficient reason to believe it. But (i) this is stated non-contrastively, and (ii) we need some idea of what it takes to have sufficient reason to believe something. Sinnott-Armstrong offers the following principle, inspired by the relevant alternatives theories of knowledge offered by Dretske (1970) and Lewis (1996):

**Ruling Out:** *s* is justified in believing that *p* out of *Q* iff *s* has sufficient reason to rule out all the other alternatives in *Q*.[19]

---

[19] Sinnott-Armstrong is also sympathetic to the idea that being justified in believing that *p* relative to *Q* requires having some positive reason to believe *p*, as well as having sufficient

It might be a bit more natural to state things in terms of having sufficient *evidence* to rule out the alternatives. But, since I'm talking about reasons, and since any piece of evidence is very plausibly a reason for belief (though it might not be true that all reasons for belief are evidence), I'm going to state things in terms of reasons. One important thing to keep in mind is that having sufficient reason to rule out some alternative $q$ does not require having conclusive reason to believe $\neg q$; it may be enough if your reasons for belief make $q$ very unlikely, for example. A second important caveat is that it isn't enough, according to this principle, to have more reason to believe $p$ than any other alternative in $Q$, since that still might not be enough to rule out the other alternatives.

Note that though this principle does relativize justification, and so whether you have sufficient reason to believe that $p$, to sets of alternatives—you might have sufficient reason to believe that $p$ relative to $Q$ but not relative to $Q'$—it does not yet make reasons contrastive. So why think that contrastivism about justification requires contrastivism about reasons? Here's a case (borrowed from Dretske, 1970) that I think illustrates the motivating idea well. Suppose you're at the zoo. You see a black and white striped horse-like animal in front of you. And suppose that this visual evidence is the only relevant reason for belief. Well, relative to the set of alternatives {believe it's a zebra, believe it's an elephant, believe it's an ostrich}, it seems that you have sufficient reason to believe it's a zebra—your reasons for belief are sufficient to rule out that it's an ostrich or an elephant. But relative to the set of alternatives {believe it's a zebra, believe it's a cleverly disguised mule}, it seems that you don't have sufficient reason to believe that it's a zebra. In fact, it looks like the fact that was your reason for belief in the previous case, that you were having such-and-such visual experience, is not even a reason in this case—the fact that you see a black and white striped horse-like animal is not a reason to believe it's a zebra rather than a cleverly disguised mule. That would certainly explain why you aren't justified relative to this new set, since justification requires having sufficient reason for belief. So here's a principle relating contrastive justification and contrastive reasons:

---

reason to rule out the alternatives. I'll ignore that addendum here, because I don't think it affects either his or my argument. It is also relevant, I think, that, since the alternatives in $Q$ are supposed to be mutually exclusive, evidence for $p$ will likely be evidence *against* the other alternatives.

**Contrastive Justification, Contrastive Reasons:** $s$ is justified in believing $p$ out of $Q$ iff $s$'s reasons for belief relative to $Q$ are sufficient to rule out every member of $Q$ except for $p$.

We can explain why justification is contrastive by pointing out that (i) justification requires having sufficient reason to believe, and (ii) reasons for belief are reasons only relative to sets of alternatives.

But is this the only, or even obviously the best, way to explain why justification is contrastive? I don't think so. Suppose that reasons aren't contrastive. Here's a story about how justification could still be contrastive. Non-contrastive reasons favor believing certain propositions independently of any set of alternatives. And, importantly, some non-contrastive reasons favor ruling out some propositions—that is, believing their negation—independently of any set of alternatives. Then we can give the following principle:

**Contrastive Justification, Non-Contrastive Reasons:** $s$ is justified in believing that $p$ out of $Q$ iff $s$ has sufficient reason to rule out all the alternatives in $Q$ except for $p$.[20]

This thesis appeals to non-contrastive reasons, but still allows justification to be contrastive. To know whether $s$ is justified in believing $p$, we still have to know what sets of alternatives we're talking about, so we know which alternatives have to be ruled out by $s$'s reasons. This principle, of course, is just the original idea captured by **Ruling Out**. Reasons weigh in favor of believing or disbelieving certain propositions, but only certain propositions are relevant in a given context.

Above I appealed to the zebra/cleverly disguised mule case to motivate thinking that reasons are contrastive. The intuition was that the fact that you're having such-and-such visual experience is a reason to believe that it's a zebra relative to {believe it's a zebra, believe it's an elephant, believe it's an ostrich}, but not relative to {believe it's a zebra, believe it's a cleverly disguised mule}. I think there's something to this claim: this kind of case does at least give us prima facie evidence that reasons are contrastive. But note that this evidence is independent of contrastivism about justification. Further, I think there is something the non-contrastivist about reasons can say to explain this kind of case: roughly, we can hold that it's true to

---

[20] We could add that $s$ needs some positive reason to believe that $p$.

say that *r* is a reason to believe that *p* when the relevant set of alternatives is *Q* only if *r* is a stronger reason to believe *p* than to believe any of the other alternatives in *Q*. Since the fact that you're having such-and-such visual experience is not a stronger reason to believe that it's a zebra than to believe that it's a cleverly disguised mule, according to this view, it's not true to say, 'It's a reason to believe it's a zebra', when believing it's a cleverly disguised mule is a relevant alternative. On the other hand, this claim would be true if the relevant alternative were, say, believing that it's an ostrich. (I'll say more about this idea in Chapter 2, and then again in Chapter 3 when I discuss the view I call *shallow contrastivism*.)

I've argued that contrastivism about justification does not require contrastivism about reasons. Now I'll argue that contrastivism about reasons does not require contrastivism about justification.

Suppose that reasons are contrastive. Further, suppose I'm a skeptic— I don't think that you can ever be justified in believing anything. I can still accept that reasons are contrastive: you might have good reason to believe that the animal is a zebra rather than an ostrich. But I just don't think this matters for justification, because to be justified in believing that it's a zebra, you have to rule out all of the possible alternative hypotheses. So the contrastive reasons that matter in determining whether you're justified in believing that it's a zebra will be {it's a zebra, it's an ostrich, it's a cleverly disguised mule, it's a hallucination,...}. And, since you don't—and couldn't—have sufficient reason to believe that it's a zebra out of this set, you aren't justified. Or perhaps I have a more moderate view of justification: I think that the set that matters in determining whether you're justified is always just what Sinnott-Armstrong (2004, 2006, 2008) calls an "everyday" contrast class, like {it's a zebra, it's an ostrich, it's an elephant}. That is, I think the skeptic makes unreasonable demands on the alternatives you have to rule out to be justified. Since you do have sufficient reason to believe that it's a zebra relative to this everyday set, your belief is justified (full stop). According to either of these views, then, reasons are contrastive, but justification is not—there is a particular, fixed set of alternatives that is relevant for determining whether or not you are justified. So, though there are reasons relative to other sets, they aren't relevant for justification.[21]

---

[21] Sinnott-Armstrong (2004, 2006) does provide arguments against these sorts of views. But the point I want to make is just that contrastivism about reasons is neither necessary

## 1.2.2 Reasons and 'ought'

Contrastivism about 'ought' is the view that 'ought' claims are always to be interpreted relative to some particular set of alternatives. Whenever an agent ought to perform some action, there is some set out of which she ought to perform it. Several writers have argued that 'ought', or what agents ought to do (to put it non-linguistically), is contrastive, for a variety of reasons. For example, Jackson (1985) points out that a contrastive theory of 'ought' lets us explain why each of the following claims seems true, even though at least some of them are incompatible with one another, assuming we aren't dealing with moral dilemmas:

1. Lucretia ought to use less painful poisons on her political enemies.
2. Lucretia ought to use painless poisons on her political enemies.
3. Lucretia ought to use political means rather than poison to achieve her ends.
4. Lucretia ought to adopt better political ends.
5. Lucretia ought to drop politics altogether and spend her days helping those in need.

Each of these can be true relative to a different set of alternatives; as we move down the list, new alternatives are introduced. A non-contrastive view of 'ought' will have trouble explaining why each of these claims is acceptable, at least before we see the later claims.

For the purposes of this section, I'll assume that contrastivism about 'ought' is well motivated. So now what I need to do is (i) sketch the relationship between 'ought' and reasons and (ii) determine whether this relationship demands that if one of the concepts is contrastive then the other is.

The most natural thesis about the relationship between 'ought' and reasons says that you ought to A iff you have most reason to A. This thesis fits nicely with an attractive picture of deliberation. To decide what you ought to do, you just weigh up all your reasons to determine which option is best supported by them; that's the one that you ought to do.[22]

---

nor sufficient for contrastivism about justification, and moreover that there are plausible views that accept contrastivism about one concept without accepting contrastivism about the other.

[22] There are complicated questions about how to determine what you have most reason to do—how reasons interact with one another. See Broome (2004), Dancy (2004), Horty (2007, 2012), and Schroeder (2007: ch. 7) for discussion about how your reasons determine

The contrastivist about 'ought', though, cannot accept it as stated, since she thinks that we need to relativize claims about what agents ought to do to sets of alternatives. And, since these alternatives need not be exhaustive, we can't simply talk about what you have most reason to do *simpliciter*, either, in trying to state the relationship between what you ought to do (relative to a certain set of alternatives) and reasons. It seems that we need to look at your reasons to do things, somehow restricted or relativized to the set of alternatives to which the 'ought' claim is relativized.

One way around this problem is to relativize reasons, as well as 'ought', to sets of alternatives—that is, to be contrastivists about reasons. This lets us retain an attractive picture of deliberation, analogous to the standard one I mentioned above. We begin with some relevant set of alternatives, Q, and then simply deliberate over the alternatives in Q. So it's easy to see why one might think that adopting contrastivism about 'ought' requires adopting contrastivism about reasons.

But this is too fast. It's possible to give a very plausible picture on which 'ought' is contrastive but reasons are not. Begin with a traditional non-contrastive picture of reasons, on which they are considerations that favor certain actions with a certain weight, some stronger or weightier than others. Collect all of the agent's reasons and weigh them up (in some way). This will give us an overall ranking of all the possible options open to the agent. We can even divide these options up as finely as you want. Maybe the resolution at which we divide them is the resolution at which the agent's intentional actions can make a difference: I can intentionally bring it about that I put between 10.55 and 10.56 gallons of gas in my car, but I can't intentionally bring it about that I put between 10.555 and 10.556 gallons, for example.[23] If that's right, then we can have one option in which I put between 10.55 gallons and 10.56 gallons in, and one in which I put between 10.56 and 10.57 gallons in. But we don't have more fine-grained options than this. This doesn't mean that I'll always deliberate between options divided up at even this high a resolution; I'll say more about that shortly.

So now what we have is an overall ranking of the possible options, according to how my reasons weigh in favor of them. In any particular

what you ought to do, or how your *pro tanto* reasons determine what you have *most* reason to do.

[23] Cf. the discussion in Kierland (2012), Cariani (2013).

context of deliberation, only some of these options will be relevant, and I'll deliberate only between those relevant options at some particular resolution. This will generate our set, $Q$. Then we can give the following principle:

> **Contrastive Ought, Non-Contrastive Reasons:** $s$ ought to $A$ out of $Q$ iff $s$ has more reason to $A$ than to perform any other alternative in $Q$.

We essentially pull out the alternatives in $Q$ from our overall ranking, retaining the order of these alternatives. Non-exhaustivity is secured, since $Q$ need not include all the options that are ranked in the original ranking. Still, the options that do make it into $Q$ will occupy a particular place on the original ranking, and the order between them will be retained in $Q$. We just appeal to this ranking, provided by my non-contrastive reasons, to determine what I ought to do.

That's non-exhaustivity. Here's how to capture resolution sensitivity. If the alternatives in $Q$ are divided up at a lower level of resolution than the options in the original ranking are—so that my reasons rank the options at a higher resolution than the resolution at which I deliberate between them—we group them in the obvious way. For example, if I'm deliberating between putting more than ten gallons of gas in the car and putting ten gallons or less in, the alternatives will be grouped in that way: {put in 10 gallons or less, put in more than 10 gallons}. We then have a few options in determining how these coarse-grained options are ranked. We could rank them based on (i) the average position of the more fine-grained alternatives they subsume, (ii) the rank of the highest or (iii) lowest fine-grained option they subsume, or (iv) the fine-grained option I would actually perform, were I to decide on the coarse-grained option. I will not try to settle which of these is best; the point is just that there are plausible ways for a contrastivist about 'ought' to retain a non-contrastive view of reasons.

Now I will argue that contrastivism about reasons is not sufficient for contrastivism about 'ought'. So, first, suppose that reasons are contrastive: a reason to $A$ is only such a reason relative to certain sets of alternatives. If we accept anything like the claim that you ought to $A$ iff you have most reason to $A$, how can we maintain a non-contrastivist view of 'ought'? Here's one way. Adopt the plausible view that you ought to $A$ iff there's more reason to $A$ than not to $A$.[24] Importing contrastivism about rea-

---

[24] This is essentially the principle that Schroeder (2007: 130–1) adopts.

sons now, even though reasons are only reasons relative to certain sets of alternatives, the particular reasons that we're concerned with in trying to decide whether you ought to A are the reasons relative to the set of alternatives, {A, ¬A}.

We could also make the set that matters for determining what you ought to do more interesting: perhaps it's determined by the things that it's possible for you to do. This doesn't amount to accepting contrastivism about 'ought', since we can just say that what you ought to do is simply the best thing you can do. According to this view, the contrastive reasons we are concerned with are the ones that are reasons relative to the set of all the things that it's possible for you to do. The central idea here is just that, when we are trying to determine what someone ought to do, we look at the reasons relative to some particular privileged set of alternatives. (This mirrors the strategy I used in the case of justification, when I introduced skeptical and everyday contrast classes.)

Contrastivism about reasons isn't idle on this picture, though. We can still appeal to the contrast-sensitivity of reasons to explain phenomena like the following, observed by Sinnott-Armstrong (2004, 2006, 2008). Today is your birthday. Suppose I'm trying to decide whether to bake you a chocolate cake, or no cake at all. Then the fact that today is your birthday is a reason to bake you a chocolate cake. But now suppose I'm trying to decide whether to bake you a chocolate cake or a lemon cake. The fact that today is your birthday seems not to be a reason to bake you a chocolate cake in this case. The contrastivist has an easy explanation: it's a reason to bake you a chocolate cake out of {bake you a chocolate cake, don't bake you any cake}, but not out of {bake you a chocolate cake, bake you a lemon cake}.[25] So there's still some motivation for adopting contrastivism about reasons, since it lets us explain these kinds of cases; it's just that, when you're trying to decide if you ought to A, you're concerned only with a certain set of your contrastive reasons: those relative to the privileged set.

I don't claim to have shown that Sinnott-Armstrong's argument to the best explanation cannot work. To salvage the argument, we would need to show that, even though contrastivism about 'ought' or justification neither requires nor is required by contrastivism about reasons, his explanation is nevertheless the *best* one. One challenge here is that the views I described that accept contrastivism about 'ought' or justification without accepting

[25] I will return to this example in Chapter 2.

contrastivism about reasons seem very reasonable, and I'm not sure what evidence we could marshal in favor of the views that accept contrastivism about both 'ought'/justification and reasons over these, beyond giving direct arguments for contrastivism about reasons. Finally, of course, for the argument actually to be compelling, we would need to establish contrastivism about 'ought' and justification. Giving direct arguments for contrastivism about reasons, on the other hand, will let us avoid holding that view hostage to the fortune of these other contrastive theories.

### 1.2.3 Reasons and explanation

In the previous two subsections, I discussed the relationship between two important normative concepts, 'ought' and justification, and normative reasons. In this subsection, I'm going to talk about the relationship between explanation and *explanatory* reasons. Moral philosophers, understandably, focus mostly on normative reasons. And, even when they talk about explanatory reasons, they are usually most interested in explanatory reasons of the motivating variety: those that explain an agent's behavior by being considerations the agent took to be normative reasons, or the reasons *for which* the agent acted. Even philosophers of science and epistemologists generally talk about explanations rather than explanatory reasons. So there's a lack of literature on the topic of explanatory reasons; everyone recognizes that there are such reasons, but few writers have had much to say about them.[26] But it's important for my purposes to explore the topic, because Sinnott-Armstrong thinks that all reasons, normative and explanatory, are contrastive.

Explanatory reasons are clearly closely related to explanations. And a prominent idea in the philosophy of science is that explanation is contrastive.[27] Contrastivism about explanation is the view that some fact $e$ explains an event, or perhaps another fact, $f$, relative only to certain sets of alternatives. For example, the fact that it's humid outside explains why it's raining rather than not precipitating, but it does not explain why it's raining rather than snowing. And the fact that it's above the freezing point explains why it's raining rather than snowing, but not why it's raining rather than not precipitating. My sense of the literature is that contrastivism about explanation is more widely accepted than contrastivism

---

[26] For a recent exception, see Skow (2016).
[27] See van Fraassen (1980), Garfinkel (1981), Lipton (1990), Hitchcock (1996).

about other concepts, such as knowledge and 'ought'. For the remainder of this section, I'll assume that contrastivism about explanation is true.

So the next step is to figure out what the relationship is between explanation and explanatory reasons. As I have already mentioned, there has not been much written about this topic. The reason for this, I suggest, is that explanatory reasons just are explanations. Explanatory reasons are usually glossed as answers to 'Why?' questions: the reason why the carpet is wet is that the roof leaked; the reason why I'm sunburnt is that I forgot to put on sunscreen. And so on. But all of these things just look like explanations of the relevant facts. One idea is that explanatory reasons are *part* of the explanation for some fact. The explanation for why I'm sunburnt is that I forgot to put on sunscreen and I stayed in the direct sunlight for a long time and my skin has certain properties and . . . Each of these individual parts of the explanation might be an explanatory reason; each explanatory reason contributes to the full explanation. The problem with this, though, is that when we cite explanatory reasons we simply seem to be giving explanations: saying 'The reason why I'm sunburnt is that I forgot to put on sunscreen' seems to be the same as saying 'The explanation for why I'm sunburnt is that I forgot to put on sunscreen'. It's plausible that we're just citing parts of explanations even when we use the word 'explanation', but the point is just that, whenever we purport to cite an explanation using 'explanation', we could just as well have used 'reason'.

If explanatory reasons just are explanations, or if to give an explanation for *p* is just to cite an explanatory reason why *p*, then obviously contrastivism about explanation entails contrastivism about explanatory reasons. So, in that sense, Sinnott-Armstrong's argument works in this case, though it doesn't seem that he had anything quite so trivial in mind. The important point to consider now, though, is whether accepting contrastivism about explanatory reasons puts pressure on us to accept contrastivism about normative reasons. I'll argue that it doesn't, at least not without some further assumptions that can be rejected.

The first strategy, and the one that Sinnott-Armstrong seems to adopt, is to say that normative reasons and explanatory reasons are simply different species of the same genus, *reasons*. There are just reasons; normative reasons and explanatory reasons are just particular kinds. But, since they're part of the same general category, important structural features, like alternative-relativity, should be shared. So, since explanatory reasons are contrastive, reasons are contrastive. And that means, on this view, that normative reasons are contrastive as well. Some support for this view comes simply from the fact that we call both normative and explanatory reasons 'reasons'. Surely this isn't an accident, and one possible explanation is that the two categories are just species of the same genus.

One problem with this view is that it seems undermotivated. The simple fact that we call both explanatory and normative reasons 'reasons' is not enough to establish that there's really just one thing, reasons, and two different kinds. This is especially so given the apparent differences—and seemingly structural differences—between explanatory and normative reasons. For example, there can be a normative reason for $s$ to $A$ even if $s$ does not $A$, but there can't be an explanatory reason why $p$ if $p$ is false. Another apparent structural difference is that explanatory reasons seem to take propositions as their complements: we give reasons why $p$ for a proposition $p$. But normative reasons appear to take actions or attitudes as their complements: we have reasons to $A$ for an action $A$, or reasons to form attitude $A$.[28] For these and other reasons, many philosophers think that there are important differences between normative reasons and explanatory reasons. Another way in which this thesis is controversial (if it is to be distinct from the next strategy that I'll consider) is that many philosophers think that normative reasons are special kinds of explanatory reasons. On the view under consideration now, we have two different species of reasons, with neither being a special case of the other (although they are of the same genus).

A second strategy is to say that normative reasons are simply a special kind of explanatory reason; that is, normative reasons are explanatory reasons that explain a normative fact. Toulmin (1950), Finlay (2001, 2006, 2014), Searle (2001), and Broome (2004) all hold some variety of this view (with important differences, of course). If normative reasons are just a special kind of explanatory reasons, and explanatory reasons are contrastive, then normative reasons are contrastive, too.

A problem with this strategy is that it is incompatible with the popular 'reasons first' approach to normativity, according to which all normative notions can be understood in terms of reasons. This is obviously not something that everyone agrees can be done, but many people do think so.

---

[28] One promising route here might be to follow Hieronymi (2005) and note that both explanatory and normative reasons are considerations that bear on a question. This might be the underlying unifying feature in virtue of which both categories count as reasons. I won't pursue this here, though.

If we analyze normative reasons as considerations that explain some normative fact, like why you ought to A, or why it would be good if you were to A, or something like that, then we cannot analyze the notion of 'ought' or of goodness in terms of reasons, on pain of circularity. Since this strategy is incompatible with such a widely held view, it is controversial (which, again, is what I want to establish here).

A third strategy is to argue that the correct analysis of normative reasons must be in terms of explanation, or of explanatory reasons. For example, perhaps for r to be a reason for you to A, it has to explain why your A-ing would promote your desires, or why it would be good in some way if you were to A. Then, if explanation is contrastive, perhaps the contrastivity will be passed on to normative reasons.[29]

But not all views of normative reasons have it that they are correctly analyzed in terms of explanation. Hampton (1998), Scanlon (1998), and Parfit (2011), for example, simply take the reason relation as primitive. It's just a (normative) fact about the world that some considerations favor some things, and explanation doesn't enter into it. And, if the correct analysis of normative reasons is not in terms of explanation, then contrastivism about explanation will not support contrastivism about reasons.

I don't claim to have offered knockdown arguments against any of these three strategies for moving from contrastivism about explanation to contrastivism about normative reasons. But I hope I have shown that all three are controversial. Just as I do not want to rely on the truth of contrastivism about 'ought' or justification to establish contrastivism about reasons—which I think is a more defensible view, anyway—I do not want to rely on these controversial accounts of the relationship between normative and explanatory reasons. In the rest of the book, I'm going to try to offer more direct evidence that reasons are contrastive.

## 1.3 The Plan

To close this chapter, I'll briefly preview the rest of the book. In Chapters 2, 3, and 4, I aim to develop a detailed and attractive version of contrastivism

---

[29] It is actually not at all straightforward to move from contrastivism about explanation, through one of these kinds of analyses, to contrastivism about reasons. But illustrating this is not necessary for the main point I want to make—that any analysis of reasons like this is controversial.

in three steps, each of which is independently motivated. After the full theory is on the table, I will illustrate other interesting applications of contrastivism in ethics, epistemology, and practical reasoning in the final two chapters.

In Chapter 2, I'll argue that our *talk* about reasons motivates a shallow kind of contrastivism—the view that the word 'reason', as used to ascribe normative reasons, expresses a relation with an argument place for sets of alternatives. The central argument will be that non-contrastive theories have trouble explaining puzzling features of explicitly contrastive reason ascriptions that employ the phrase 'rather than'. So the first step is to motivate and develop a contrastive account of our talk about reasons.

But this leaves open a view, which I call *shallow contrastivism*, on which contrastivity goes only language-deep. According to this view, though the word 'reason' expresses a relation with an argument place for sets of alternatives, that relation is *not* the important normative relation for theorizing in ethics, epistemology, and practical reasoning. There is an underlying non-contrastive normative *favoring* relation that holds between actions or attitudes and considerations which favor them independently of the relevant alternatives, and in terms of which we can analyze the contrastive relation expressed by 'reason'. This is a more conservative view than *deep contrastivism*, according to which the contrastive relation expressed by 'reason' is the important normative relation, and is not to be analyzed in terms of a deeper non-contrastive normative relation. However, after sketching shallow contrastivism, I'll argue that the normative favoring relation itself is contrastive, so that we should adopt deep contrastivism. This is the second step in developing contrastivism.

The theory, as it stands after Chapter 3, is that reasons to $A$, out of a set of alternatives $Q$, are facts that favor $A$-ing out of $Q$. This is just the contrastivist implementation of the ubiquitous, if uninformative, view that reasons are considerations that favor the things they are reasons for. The third step is to try to say something more substantive, by giving an analysis of the favoring, or reason, relation. In fact, I'll show that we need to do this, since otherwise contrastivism faces a serious problem. The problem is one that faces us if we let our contrastivism go too deep—that is, if we don't *constrain* the contrast-sensitivity of reasons. I will argue, however, that we can solve this problem by appealing to the popular idea that reasons involve the *promotion* of various kinds of objectives, like desires or values. And, moreover, I'll argue that this idea itself provides strong independent support for contrastivism, since contrastivism provides the best way to understand how reasons could involve promotion. The result, I argue, is an attractive *moderate* version of contrastivism about reasons.

In Chapter 5, I'll consider the possibility of the intransitivity of 'more reason than'. Most people think this relation couldn't possibly be intransitive, but others, such as Temkin (1987, 2012), Rachels (1998, 2001), and Friedman (2009), have given compelling arguments for the possibility of intransitivity. From this perspective, contrastivism might seem especially well placed to accommodate and explain intransitivity, in virtue of the independence of reasons relative to different alternatives. I'll explore ways we might do just that, and conclude that contrastivism does in fact provide an especially natural framework on which to accommodate intransitivity, but that doing so is ultimately optional for the contrastivist.

Finally, in Chapter 6, I'll use contrastivism to provide an attractive account of rational withholding of both belief and intention—an important but underexplored topic in the theory of rationality. The upshot of these final two chapters is that contrastivism about reasons has interesting applications in normative domains, in which reasons are of fundamental importance.

# 2

# Reason Claims

Now that I've gotten the preliminaries on the table, and argued that to establish contrastivism we need some *direct* evidence that reasons are contrastive, I'll start trying to provide that evidence. In this chapter, I'll argue that our talk about reasons—our use of what I'll call *reason claims*—supports contrastivism. There are puzzles involving various sorts of claims that are best solved by contrastivism.

## 2.1 A Simple Argument

Sinnott-Armstrong (2004, 2006, 2008) observes that the following reason ascriptions may both be intuitively true in the same situation:

(1) The fact that it's your birthday is a reason for me to bake you a chocolate cake rather than bake you no cake at all.
(2) The fact that it's your birthday is not a reason for me to bake you a chocolate cake rather than bake you a lemon cake.

So it seems that whether the fact that it is your birthday is a reason for me to bake you a chocolate cake or not depends on what we are comparing that action to—relative to some alternatives, it is, and relative to others, it is not. Sinnott-Armstrong concludes that reasons are always reasons for one thing *rather than* another: to know whether some fact is a reason for some action, we have to know 'rather than what?'. That is, 'reason' expresses a relation with an argument place for an alternative, or set of alternatives, relative to which the consideration is a reason for the action. This easily explains how (1) and (2) could both be true: the 'rather than' clause makes explicit the alternative relative to which the fact that it's your birthday is or is not a reason for me to bake you a chocolate cake.

This argument for contrastivism, however, is too fast. First, contrastivism holds that *all* reasons are contrastive. But most reason ascriptions are not explicitly contrastive, unlike (1) and (2). So one way we may resist contrastivism, in the face of Sinnott-Armstrong's observation, is to hold that 'reason' is ambiguous between a contrastive sense and a non-contrastive sense. The contrastive sense is used in claims like (1) and (2), while the non-contrastive sense is used in non-contrastive ascriptions, like 'The fact that it's your birthday is a reason for me to bake you a chocolate cake'.

I think this view is unattractive, because 'reason' fails a standard test for ambiguity, which Schaffer (2007) has called *coordination across conjunction*, or the *conjunction reduction* test. Consider the word 'light', which has (at least) two different meanings, illustrated by 'The colors are light' and 'The feathers are light'. To see that there are two different meanings for 'light' here, we can conjoin these two sentences, but use 'light' only once so that it is required to latch on to both conjuncts. If the result is infelicitous, then that's some evidence that 'light' is ambiguous. So consider 'The colors and the feathers are light'. This sentence is clearly odd, at least on the interpretation where it's a conjunction of the most natural readings of the previous two sentences. That's evidence that 'light' is ambiguous between these two sentences.

On the other hand, consider another term that some have thought is ambiguous, 'exist'. One might think that there are two meanings of 'exist' such that, on one meaning, 'Chairs exist' is true, while, on another, 'Numbers exist' is true. To test whether we might have two meanings here, consider the conjunction, 'Chairs and numbers exist'. This sentence seems perfectly felicitous when interpreted as a conjunction of the previous two sentences. This is evidence that 'exist' is not ambiguous between these two sentences.[1]

'Reason' fails this test for ambiguity (at least ambiguity between a contrastive and a non-contrastive sense) because sentences like the following are perfectly appropriate:

(3) The fact that you sprained your ankle is a reason to wear your brace, and to lift weights rather than run.

---

[1] I borrow these examples from Sennet (2015).

Again, there is just one occurrence of 'reason' here; this suggests that 'reason' latches on to both conjuncts, 'to wear your brace' and 'to lift weights rather than run'. The first conjunct, though, is non-contrastive, while the second is explicitly contrastive. If the single occurrence of 'reason' latches on to both conjuncts, that is evidence that 'reason' is univocal, whether it takes a contrastive or a non-contrastive complement. While this test is not conclusive, it does give us some good evidence that 'reason' is not ambiguous between a contrastive and a non-contrastive sense. So sentences like (3) are a problem for the ambiguity view.[2]

Ruling out the ambiguity view, though, does not yet establish contrastivism. We can still try to offer non-contrastive analyses of explicitly contrastive reason ascriptions like (1) and (2). If we can analyze these sentences in terms of non-contrastive reasons, then they will not cause a problem for the non-contrastivist.

A tempting, but ultimately problematic, idea is to give an analysis in terms of the strength of reasons, like one of the following:

RT-1:   $r$ is a reason to $A$ rather than $B$ iff $r$ is a stronger reason to $A$ than it is to $B$.

RT-2:   $r$ is a reason to $A$ rather than $B$ iff $r$ is either (i) a stronger reason to $A$ than it is to $B$, or (ii) a stronger reason not to $B$ than it is not to $A$.

Either of these analyses would let us explain how (1) and (2) could both be true without resorting to contrastivism. Since the fact that it's your birthday is a stronger reason to bake you a chocolate cake than to bake you no cake at all, (1) is true, according to either analysis. But, since this fact is an equally strong reason to bake you a chocolate cake and to bake you a lemon cake, (2) is also true, according to either analysis.

While these analyses do seem natural, I think both face a serious problem. The problem is that they require the phrase 'rather than' to function very differently in reason ascriptions than it functions in other contexts. In ordinary uses of 'rather than', like 'I want pizza rather than salad', 'Bob went to the store rather than to the gym', and 'Two plus two equals four rather than five', 'rather than' seems to mean something along the lines of 'and not', perhaps with an implicature that the two things being contrasted

---

[2] See Schaffer (2007: 396).

are somehow especially relevant.³ But according to RT-1 and RT-2, 'rather than', as used in reason ascriptions, does not mean anything like 'and not', but instead means 'stronger than'. So they seem to rely on an ad hoc treatment of 'rather than' in reason ascriptions. This is a serious cost for these proposals.

Nevertheless, I do agree that there is something compelling about this kind of proposal. To anticipate, the contrastive view I develop in Chapter 4 is in one way similar to these analyses. But my view appeals to the idea of a ranking in the account of what it is for some consideration to be a reason, instead of in the analysis of 'rather than' reason ascriptions. This allows the view in Chapter 4 to treat 'rather than' as having the same kind of meaning in reason ascriptions as it has elsewhere.

Some writers, in objecting to contrastivism about explanation and about knowledge, have given non-contrastivist analyses of explicitly contrastive claims on which 'rather than' does mean 'and not'.⁴ Consider the following two proposals, which adopt this strategy, and differ only in the scope of the 'not':

RT-3:  $r$ is a reason to $A$ rather than $B$ iff $r$ is a reason to $A$ and $r$ is not a reason to $B$.

RT-4:  $r$ is a reason to $A$ rather than $B$ iff $r$ is a reason to $A$ and $r$ is a reason not to $B$.

Either of these proposals lets us explain how (1) and (2) could both be true, without resorting to contrastivism. Since the fact that it's your birthday is both a reason to bake you a chocolate cake and a reason to bake you a lemon cake, (2) is true according to either proposal. And, since this fact is not a reason to bake you no cake at all, and in fact a reason *not* to bake you no cake at all, (1) is also true according to either proposal.

Since there are reasonable, independently motivated non-contrastivist explanations of the data provided by (1) and (2), Sinnott-Armstrong is too quick in concluding on this basis that reasons are contrastive. What

---

³ 'Rather than' as used in preference ascriptions may seem to fit better with RT-1 and RT-2: 'I prefer cake rather than pie' might seem to mean that I like cake more than I like pie. But it should be uncontroversial that preference is a contrastive notion—it may imply these kinds of claims about liking, but it need not be analyzed in this way.

⁴ See Ruben (1987), Temple (1988) for this sort of strategy in resisting contrastivism about explanation. See Schaffer (2008) for arguments against this kind of analysis of 'rather than' knowledge ascriptions, and Rickless (2014) for further discussion.

ascriptions like (1) and (2) do show, however, is that non-contrastivists need to say *something* about these explicitly contrastive ascriptions; I've argued in this section that they should take some version of the popular anti-contrastivist strategy, treating 'rather than' as meaning (roughly) 'and not'. But now that we've seen this, we're in a position to give a stronger argument for contrastivism.

## 2.2 A Stronger Argument

### 2.2.1 *The argument*

Suppose that I need to get to campus sometime today, but live twenty miles away. Further, suppose I'm out of shape and don't want to wear myself out getting there. Now consider the following reason ascriptions:

(4) The fact that campus is twenty miles away is a reason to drive to campus rather than bike there.

(5) The fact that campus is twenty miles away is a reason to bike to campus rather than run there.

Both of these sentences are intuitively true, given the set-up of the case. But, as I'll now show, this causes problems for the non-contrastivist.

First, notice that it follows from both RT-3 and RT-4 that, if '$r$ is a reason for $A$ rather than $B$' is true, then $r$ is a reason for $A$.[5] So, on both proposed analyses, (6) follows from (5):

(6) The fact that campus is twenty miles away is a reason to bike to campus.

Since (6) follows from (5) on both proposals, and since (5) is true, the non-contrastivist is committed to the truth of (6).

Now consider RT-3, which says that we should analyze '$r$ is a reason to $A$ rather than $B$' as saying that $r$ is a reason to $A$ and $r$ is not a reason to $B$. According to this view, (7) follows from (4):

(7) The fact that campus is twenty miles away is not a reason to bike to campus.

---

[5] This also plausibly follows from RT-1, since, if $r$ is a stronger reason for $A$ than it is for $B$, it is surely a reason for $A$. This does not follow from RT-2. But, as I argued in Section 2.1, RT-2 (as well as RT-1) relies on an idiosyncratic treatment of 'rather than' in reason ascriptions.

The problem, of course, is that (6) and (7), both of which the non-contrastivist who adopts RT-3 is committed to, are inconsistent. So this analysis of 'rather than' ascriptions fails.

Now consider RT-4, on which '$r$ is a reason to $A$ rather than $B$' means that $r$ is a reason to $A$ and $r$ is a reason not to $B$. This view also leads to a problem, though not to an outright contradiction. For, on that proposal, (8)—instead of (7)—follows from (4):

(8) The fact that campus is twenty miles away is a reason not to bike to campus.

The non-contrastivist who adopts RT-4 is thus committed to both (6) and (8); that is, she is committed to saying that the fact that campus is twenty miles away is both a reason *to* bike to campus and a reason *not to* bike to campus. But this is an implausible result. So the second proposal, while not leading to an outright contradiction, does give us an implausible result.

## 2.2.2 Response: denying exclusivity

The non-contrastivist may question the implausibility of the result, that the fact that campus is twenty miles away is both a reason to bike there and a reason not to bike there. If this result isn't really troubling, then the argument against RT-4 is no good. So why think it is troubling?

One reason that many people will find this result implausible is that it violates the following principle:

**Exclusivity:** For all facts $r$, agents $s$, and actions $A$, if $r$ is a reason for $s$ to $A$, then it's not the case that $r$ is also a reason for $s$ not to $A$.

Philosophers who seem to accept this principle include Nagel (1970), Raz (1999), and Crisp (2000). If **Exclusivity** is true, then the argument I've given shows that none of the non-contrastivist analyses of 'rather than' ascriptions that I've considered so far could be correct.

But in fact there's reason to question **Exclusivity**. Jonathan Dancy has argued that the principle is false by appealing to cases like the following.[6] Suppose I love to talk to famous people, but hate to be snubbed. And suppose that, unfortunately, famous people are likely to snub guys like

---

[6] See Dancy (1993: 62) for discussion.

me. Then the fact that the person across the bar is famous is a reason for me to go to talk to her, since I love to talk to famous people. But it's also a reason for me not to go to talk to her, since I hate to be snubbed, and since famous people are likely to snub guys like me. If this is the right way to describe this case (and I think it is), then **Exclusivity** is false.

Further, common theories of reasons seem committed to the falsity of **Exclusivity**. On a simple desire-based theory of reasons, for example, when you have a desire that $A$-ing would help promote, and $r$ explains why this is so, $r$ is a reason to $A$.[7] So, if you have *two* desires, such that $r$ explains both why $A$-ing would promote one of them and why not $A$-ing would promote the other, this kind of theory entails that $r$ is both a reason for you to $A$ and a reason for you not to $A$. Similarly, on a standard value-based theory, all we need is a case in which there are two values such that $r$ explains both why $A$-ing would promote or respect one of them and why not $A$-ing would promote or respect the other.

This lets us see where **Exclusivity** goes wrong. It is common ground between desire-based and value-based theories that our reasons for action are provided or explained by various objectives—desires on the desire-based theory and values on the value-based theory (and perhaps both on a hybrid theory). When a fact $r$ helps explain why my $A$-ing would promote or respect one of these objectives, $r$ is a reason for me to $A$, which is provided by that objective.[8] The problem with **Exclusivity** is that, on most theories, there are multiple objectives that can provide reasons—agents have multiple desires, and several kinds of values are worth promoting or respecting. In the case involving the famous person, for example, I have two relevant desires: first, a desire to talk to famous people, and, second, a desire not to be snubbed. The first desire explains why the fact that she's famous is a reason to go to talk to her: this fact explains why doing so would promote my desire to talk to famous people. Similarly, this same fact explains why not going to talk to her would promote my desire not to be snubbed. It is easy to construct a similar case in which multiple values, rather than multiple desires, are involved.

---

[7] See Schroeder (2007), for example.

[8] For discussion of objectives providing reasons, see Moore (1912) (though he talked about rightness rather than reasons); Nagel (1970), Anderson (1993), Scanlon (1998), Finlay (2001, 2006), Schroeder (2007), Wedgwood (2009), Parfit (2011). For analyses of reasons in terms of explanation, see Toulmin (1950), Finlay (2001, 2006), Searle (2001), Broome (2004), Schroeder (2007). I will return to this idea in Chapter 4.

What this shows is that popular theories of reasons allow for different objectives to explain why one and the same fact can be both a reason to $A$ and a reason not to $A$. But they do not allow for one and the same objective to explain why one and the same fact is both a reason to do and not to do one and the same action. That's because one fact $r$ can't explain both (i) why $A$-ing would promote or respect an objective $o$, and (ii) why not $A$-ing would also promote or respect $o$.

To illustrate this, consider Schroeder's Hypotheticalism (2007). He holds that $r$ is a reason for $s$ to $A$ iff $r$ explains why $A$-ing would promote $p$, where $p$ is the object of one of $s$'s desires, and where promoting $p$ is just making $p$ more probable. But it would be strange to think that $r$ could explain both why $A$-ing would make $p$ more probable, and why not $A$-ing would also make $p$ more probable. Similarly, it doesn't seem that one fact could explain both why $A$-ing would respect, say, the demands of justice, and why not $A$-ing would also respect the demands of justice.[9]

So the following weaker principle is very plausibly true, even if **Exclusivity** is false:

> **Restricted Exclusivity:** For all facts $r$, agents $s$, actions $A$, and objectives $o$, $o$ cannot explain both why $r$ is a reason for $s$ to $A$ and why $r$ is a reason for $s$ not to $A$.

What this principle rules out is that one and the same objective can explain why one and the same fact is both a reason to $A$ and a reason not to $A$. The cases that seem to violate **Exclusivity**, like the case of the famous person at the bar, do not violate this principle. And, as I have argued, while popular theories of reasons may allow for violations of **Exclusivity**, they do not allow for violations of **Restricted Exclusivity**.

Crucially, this principle is enough for my argument, because the joint truth of (6) and (8) *does* violate **Restricted Exclusivity**. The objective that provides, or explains, both of them is my desire not to wear myself out getting to campus. This explains both why the fact that campus is twenty

---

[9] An anonymous referee offers a case in which performing an action $A$ would *promote* a value, but not performing $A$ would *respect* the value. Torching the ballot box would rig the election in favor of the pro-democracy candidate, which would promote the value of democracy. But it would not respect it, since it would in fact undermine democracy in this case. The argument of this chapter can still go through with the even weaker claim that one and the same objective can't explain why one and the same fact is both a reason to $A$ and a reason not to $A$ *via the same relation* (i.e., promotion or respect).

miles away is a reason to drive rather than bike, and why this fact is a reason to bike rather than run. And, since these 'rather than' ascriptions, according to the non-contrastivist who adopts RT-4, are to be analyzed partly in terms of the non-contrastive reasons mentioned in (6) and (8), this single desire also explains the reasons ascribed in both (6) and (8). Thus, RT-4 leads to an implausible violation of **Restricted Exclusivity**. So 'rather than' ascriptions do ultimately cause problems for a standard non-contrastive picture of reasons, once we focus on the right kind of case.

## 2.3 Contrastivism

Now I am ready to begin to develop contrastivism about reasons. The first step is to develop a contrastive account of 'reason'-talk, motivated by the problems non-contrastive theories have with 'rather than' ascriptions.

### 2.3.1 A contrastive account of reason claims

Contrastivism differs from traditional non-contrastive theories by claiming that the reason relation includes an argument place for sets of alternatives. So the relation holds between (at least) (i) some fact $r$ which is the reason, (ii) the particular alternative $A$ which the fact is said to be a reason for, and (iii) the relevant set of alternatives *out of which* $r$ is said to be a reason for $A$. Arguably the reason relation also includes an argument place for an agent, but in what follows I will largely ignore this.

In an explicit 'rather than' ascription like 'The fact that today is your birthday is a reason to bake you a chocolate cake rather than not bake you a cake', the alternatives are provided explicitly: {bake you a chocolate cake, don't bake you a cake}.[10] These kinds of ascriptions, according to contrastivism, provide the model for all reason ascriptions. But most reason ascriptions aren't like this; most are what I'll call 'bare ascriptions', like 'The fact that it's your birthday is a reason to bake you a chocolate cake'. Since the relation that serves as the content of reason ascriptions—say, $R(r, A, Q)$—has an argument place for a set of alternatives $Q$, this set must be provided somehow before we can evaluate the ascription. As discussed in Chapter 1, the most natural way to develop the theory, and

---

[10] The set of alternatives might be larger than just two members, but, since I've been dealing with 'rather than' ascriptions here, I'll mostly limit my discussion to two-member sets.

the way I'll adopt, is to let the set of alternatives be provided by the context of utterance.[11] In a context in which a reason ascription is made, some particular set will be relevant. One straightforward way in which a set of alternatives might count as the relevant one is by including the options under discussion.[12]

We can follow linguists like Roberts (2012) and philosophers of language like Cariani (2013) in appealing to a *question under discussion*, and in particular a *deliberative* question under discussion, in a given context. These questions are standardly thought of as sets of alternatives—potential answers to the question—and certain kinds of expressions can be interpreted only once this question is supplied. This device has proved useful for several different aspects of a theory of communication, including the interpretation of focus (like intonational stress) and the notion of a *topic* of conversation. Here I am suggesting that it may also be useful in the interpretation of reason ascriptions, by supplying the set of alternatives to which the reason is relativized.[13]

Since an explicit 'rather than' ascription gives the set of alternatives explicitly, these ascriptions will have a stable content across contexts (assuming there are no other context-sensitive terms). But, since bare ascriptions have the set of alternatives provided by context, their content will shift across contexts. Here are the semantic principles I propose:

**Explicit Ascriptions:** '$r$ is a reason to $A$ rather than $B$' is true in context $c^{14}$ iff $r$ is a reason to $A$ out of $\{A, B\}$.

**Bare Ascriptions:** '$r$ is a reason to $A$' is true in context $c$ iff $r$ is a reason to $A$ out of $Q$, where $Q$ is the relevant set of alternatives in $c$.

---

[11] We might develop a theory on which it's provided instead by the context of assessment, or perhaps by some features of the agent's situation (though to count as a contrastivist theory, it should not always simply be the set of alternatives that it is possible for the agent to perform). Sinnott-Armstrong (2004, 2006) defends a view on which there's no saying which set is relevant for evaluating any particular bare reason ascription, which leads him to adopt Pyrrhonian skepticism, and thus to refuse to evaluate any bare ascription as either true or false.

[12] In Chapter 1 I also discussed the role of intonational stress in indicating the relevant alternatives.

[13] Cariani (2013) appeals to deliberative questions under discussion to develop his broadly contrastivist view of 'ought' ascriptions; see also Finlay and Snedegar (2014).

[14] Note that 'in context $c$' doesn't show up on the right-hand side of the biconditional. That's because, as I said, explicit ascriptions are not context-sensitive (at least not due to the occurrence of 'reason', unless 'reason' is context-sensitive along some further dimension).

**Bare Against Ascriptions:** '$r$ is a reason not to $A$' is true in context $c$ iff $r$ is a reason not to $A$ out of $Q$, where $Q$ is the relevant set of alternatives in $c$.[15]

Now I'll show how to use this account to explain the problematic case from the previous section.

### 2.3.2 A contrastive solution

One way to think about the problem facing the non-contrastivist is that, no matter what analysis of 'rather than' ascriptions we considered, we always derived that $r$ is a reason to $A$ from '$r$ is a reason to $A$ rather than $B$'.[16] This result, when combined with claims about $B$ that we could also derive (and that are independently plausible anyway), led either to outright contradiction or to otherwise implausible results. So the culprit seems to be this inference:

**RT:** If $r$ is a reason to $A$ rather than $B$, then $r$ is a reason to $A$.

The trouble is that this inference seems very hard to reject for the non-contrastivist.

The contrastivist, on the other hand, can not only reject this inference, but can explain why it seems so natural. Note first that RT is, of course, a non-contrastivist principle—there is no mention of contrasts on the right-hand side. So I suggest that we replace it with this:

**CRT:** If $r$ is a reason to $A$ rather than $B$, then $r$ is a reason to $A$ out of $\{A, B\}$ and $r$ is a reason not to $B$ out of $\{A, B\}$.

The second half of the consequent is perhaps less obvious than the first, but I think it is nevertheless very compelling. Given that $A$ and $B$ are mutually exclusive (why else would we use 'rather than'?), $B$-ing precludes

---

[15] If we can think of reasons against an option $A$ simply as reason for $\neg A$, then this clause is just a special case of **Bare Ascriptions**. I agree that this is an attractive view, though things are more complicated for the contrastivist, since $\neg A$ will not necessarily be in the same set of alternatives as $A$—sets of alternatives need not be *exhaustive* in this sense. And it's not clear how to make sense of a reason to $\neg A$ out of a set of alternatives that doesn't contain $\neg A$. I return to this point in Chapter 4. Further, some philosophers have recently given accounts on which reasons against $A$ cannot simply be thought of as reasons for $\neg A$. See Greenspan (2005), for example.

[16] Again, RT-2 does not validate this inference, which is an advantage of that proposal. But it does rely on a problematic treatment of 'rather than' in reason ascriptions.

*A*-ing. So, if *r* is a reason to *A* out of {*A*, *B*}, it is very plausible that it's also a reason not to *B* out of this set.[17]

Importantly, given **Bare Ascriptions**, we can now see why RT seems so natural: it's because, on the default interpretation of the consequent, RT expresses a truth. The antecedent, '*r* is a reason to *A* rather than *B*', makes salient the set of alternatives {*A*, *B*}. And according to **Bare Ascriptions**, when we interpret the consequent, '*r* is a reason to *A*' relative to this set, it means that *r* is a reason to *A* out of {*A*, *B*}. Finally, according to CRT, this will be true as long as '*r* is a reason to *A* rather than *B*'—the antecedent of RT—is true.

The mistake, though, is to move from the truth of '*r* is a reason to *A*' in the context set up by the antecedent of RT to the truth of this claim in *every* context. If the relevant set of alternatives is not the one provided by the antecedent, {*A*, *B*}, then we have no guarantee that '*r* is a reason to *A*' will be true, relative to this new set.

This puts us in a position to see how the contrastivist can solve the puzzle. First, here are the relevant sentences, rewritten to make the contrasts explicit.

(4*) The fact that campus is twenty miles away is a reason to drive rather than bike (out of {drive, bike}).
(5*) The fact that campus is twenty miles away is a reason to bike rather than run (out of {bike, run}).
(6*) The fact that campus is twenty miles away is a reason to bike (out of {bike, run}).
(8*) The fact that campus is twenty miles away is a reason not to bike (out of {drive, bike}).

The truth of the 'rather than' claim (4), along with CRT, tells us that (8) is true in a context in which the relevant set of alternatives is {drive, bike}, so we interpret (8) as (8*). But in this context, by **Bare Ascriptions**, (6) would be true only if the fact that campus is twenty miles away is a reason to bike relative to this same set:

---

[17] This shows that my view does respect the fact that 'rather than' means something like 'and not': relative to the set of alternatives {*A*, *B*}, when '*r* is a reason to *A* rather than *B*' is true, *r* is a reason to *A and* a reason *not* to *B*. I will have more to say about this idea in Chapter 4.

(6′) The fact that campus is twenty miles away is a reason to bike (out of {drive, bike}).

But this is false. So in the context in which (8) is true, (6) is false.

The truth of the 'rather than' claim (5), along with CRT, tells us that (6) is true in a context in which the relevant set of alternatives is {bike, run}, so we interpret (6) as (6*). But in this context, by **Bare Against Ascriptions**, (8) would be true only if the fact that campus is twenty miles away is a reason not to bike relative to this same set:

(8′) The fact that campus is twenty miles away is a reason not to bike (out of {bike, run}).

But this is false. So in the context in which (6) is true, (8) is false.

Thus, there's no one context in which both (6) and (8) are true—at least not one in which both reasons are provided by my desire not to wear myself out getting to campus.[18] It's true, of course, that (4) and (5) are true in the same contexts, but that's not puzzling—no one should deny that these 'rather than' claims can be jointly true. The key to the contrastivist solution is, essentially, treating all reason ascriptions as (at least implicitly) 'rather than' ascriptions—as relative to sets of alternatives.

## 2.4 Other 'Rather than' Ascriptions

I proposed the following view of when one consideration is a reason to $A$ rather than $B$:

**CRT:** If $r$ is a reason to $A$ rather than $B$, then $r$ is a reason to $A$ out of $\{A, B\}$ and $r$ is a reason not to $B$ out of $\{A, B\}$.

I suggested that, where $A$ and $B$ are mutually exclusive, if $r$ is a reason for $A$ out of $\{A, B\}$, it is also a reason against $B$—a reason not to $B$. But

---

[18] What is the status of **Restricted Exclusivity**? It's a non-contrastivist principle, so I need to reject it. But I relied on it in my argument against the non-contrastivist. I claim that the non-contrastivist is committed to this principle, which is why the case I presented in Section 2.2 is problematic for her. The contrastivist should replace **Restricted Exclusivity** with a contrastive version, which says that one and the same objective can't explain why one and the same fact is a reason to do and not to do one and the same action *relative to* one and the same set of alternatives.

there seem to be some 'rather than' reason ascriptions for which this does not hold.[19]

Suppose you think that the fact that Emmy is funny is a reason to hire her. I might reply that the fact that she's funny is a reason to socialize with her rather than hire her. According to CRT, this means that the fact that she's funny is a reason to socialize with her and a reason not to hire her—a reason *against* hiring her. But this is not what I mean: I don't think that the fact that she's funny is a reason not to hire her, I just don't think that it is a reason to hire her.

I believe this case shows that there are at least two ways to read 'rather than' reason ascriptions, and that my view, CRT, captures only one of them. A clue here is that, in the case in question, socializing with Emmy and hiring her are not mutually exclusive. So, as we will see in Chapter 4, my view does not commit me to holding that the fact that she's funny is a reason not to hire her just because it's a reason to socialize with her. In fact, since contrastivism requires that the options in a set of alternatives are mutually exclusive, we won't actually end up with a set of alternatives like {hire her, socialize with her}.

We should instead understand 'The fact that she's funny is a reason to socialize with her rather than hire her' as meaning something like this:

- The fact that she's funny is a reason to socialize with her and it's not a reason to hire her.

What we're contrasting here is the whole ascription, 'The fact that she's funny is a reason to hire her'. I am saying that this is not true, and instead that something else is true—that it's a reason to socialize with her. Of course, as a contrastivist, I have to provide sets of alternatives for the reasons ascribed. For example,

- The fact that she's funny is a reason to socialize with her (out of {socialize with her, ignore her}) and it's not a reason to hire her (out of {hire her, hire someone else}).

This may seem ad hoc, but I don't believe that it is. There is an intuitive difference between cases like the ones I appealed to—for example, 'The fact that campus is twenty miles away is a reason to drive rather than

---

[19] Thanks to a referee for Oxford University Press for this objection.

bike—and examples like this. The most important difference is that in the cases I appealed to, the options were mutually exclusive, whereas in this case, they are not. If hiring Emmy and socializing with her were mutually exclusive, then this case would be like those I appealed to, and I would insist that, *if* the fact that she's funny is a reason for socializing with her (which is incompatible with hiring her), it is a reason against hiring her (which is incompatible with socializing with her). I will return to this issue in Chapter 4.

The important point is that my view does not give us an account of every kind of 'rather than' reason ascription. In particular, it does not give us an account of such ascriptions where the two options are not mutually exclusive. In these cases, my hypothesis is that we are contrasting the whole ascription, rather than the relevant actions, as I have suggested. This is all compatible with contrastivism.

## 2.5 Negative Reason Existentials

The contrastive account of reason ascriptions I've just developed is directly motivated by the puzzle about 'rather than' ascriptions, since it takes those ascriptions as its model. What I am going to argue now is that, once we have this contrastive account in hand, we can solve a puzzle about a different kind of reason claim, *negative reason existentials*. These are claims like 'There's no reason to cry over spilled milk'. These sorts of claims are also very common, and play an important role in arguments against various theories in ethics, epistemology, and practical reasoning: some theory implies that there is a reason to A, but intuitively there is no reason to A, so the theory is false. Schroeder (2007) argues, though, that our intuitions about negative reason existentials are not to be trusted. After presenting the puzzle, I will argue that a contrastive solution is more attractive than Schroeder's own solution.

### 2.5.1 *The puzzle*

Consider the following famous case.

> THE BOOK THIEF. You see Tom Grabit run out of the library, pull a book from under his coat, cackle gleefully, and then run away.[20]

---

[20] Lehrer and Paxson (1969).

Intuitively, you have a reason to believe that Tom Grabit stole the book. But now consider this variation:

> THE TWIN BOOK THIEF.   You see Tom Grabit run out of the library, pull a book from under his coat, cackle gleefully, and then run away. Just as you begin to form the belief that Tom stole the book, your friend tells you about Tom's twin brother, Tim. Tom and Tim are indistinguishable, even to their mother.

Imagine that we've hauled Tom into the police station and charged him with stealing the book. He protests, "Wait! I have a twin brother! You have no reason to think I'm the one who stole the book!". His protest certainly seems warranted. So intuitively, in this case, you have no reason to believe that Tom stole the book. The reason provided by your visual evidence is *undercut*. And, it seems, when a reason is undercut, it's just not a reason anymore. But Schroeder argues that our intuitive judgment that there is no reason for you to believe that Tom stole the book in this case is mistaken. For consider the following variation:

> THE TRIPLET BOOK THIEF.   You see Tom Grabit run out of the library, pull a book from under his coat, cackle gleefully, and then run away. Just as you begin to form the belief that Tom stole the book, your friend tells you about Tom's two identical siblings, Tim and Tam. The triplets are indistinguishable, even to their mother.

Intuitively you have even *less* reason to believe that Tom stole the book in this case than you did in THE TWIN BOOK THIEF. But, if you have even less reason in this case, you couldn't have had *no* reason in the previous case. So our intuition that you had no reason is mistaken. This is the puzzle about negative reason existentials: some of them are intuitively true, though we also seem to be committed to the existence of the very reasons that are said not to exist.[21]

### 2.5.2 *The pragmatic solution*

Schroeder offers a pragmatic solution to this puzzle. According to this solution, the intuitively true negative reason existentials, like 'There's no reason to believe that Tom stole the book', are in fact false, but there is a pragmatic explanation for why they sound true. The central idea is that

[21] See Schroeder (2007: 93).

(i) citing normative reasons in the context of deliberation conversationally implicates that the reasons are relatively weighty ones, but (ii) the reasons in the relevant examples are in fact very weak.

This pragmatic story is easiest to understand by first focusing on a different example of Schroeder's. Suppose I tell you that you have a reason to eat your car. Initially, of course, this sounds crazy—*of course* you don't have a reason to eat your car. But Schroeder argues that this is not so obvious. In contexts of deliberation—the contexts in which we most often cite normative reasons—citing very weak reasons is irrelevant, and thus conversationally inappropriate, by Gricean maxims (Grice, 1989). We are therefore reluctant to interpret someone who ascribes a reason to us, as in 'You have a reason to eat your car', as talking about a very weak reason. As a result, there is a conversational implicature, generated by a maxim of relevance, that the reason is relatively weighty. So, if the reason is *not* weighty, the implicature is false, which can mislead us into thinking that the reason claim itself is false. If this is right, then we should predict that, by telling you that the reason in question is very weak, I can make the claim sound less crazy, since this would cancel the false implicature. So consider: you have a reason to eat your car, but it's a really weak reason, easily outweighed by all the reasons not to eat your car. This plausibly sounds less crazy than simply telling you that you have a reason to eat your car.

Schroeder also holds that, by making the bare existential claim 'You have a reason to eat your car', rather than actually saying what the reason is, I reinforce the problematic implicature. This is because the bare existential claim is less informative than actually telling you what the reason is; so, in order for the claim to be sufficiently informative to be relevant and appropriate, Schroeder holds that the reason in question must be relatively weighty. This predicts that, by telling you what the reason is, I can make the claim sound better. So consider: the fact that your car contains the recommended daily dose of iron is a reason for you to eat your car. This sounds better than the bare existential claim, as predicted. And of course it sounds better still if I follow this up with '. . . but this is a very weak reason'.

So we have a pragmatic explanation for why it can sound false to say that you have a reason to eat your car, even if there is in fact such a reason, as long as this reason is weak. It then seems to be a short step to explaining why a negative reason existential, like 'You have no reason to eat your car', or 'There's no reason to believe that Tom Grabit stole the book', could sound true, even if there is in fact a reason in these cases. Since the reasons in question are so weak, it would sound false to say that there is a reason in these cases, and so it is reasonable to think it would sound true to say that there is not a reason.[22] Consideration of THE TRIPLET BOOK THIEF seemed to show that there in fact is a reason to believe Tom stole the book in THE TWIN BOOK THIEF. But this reason is plausibly weak—it is partially undercut by the fact that Tom has a twin brother—so it sounds true to say that there is no such reason.

However, for this case actually to support Schroeder's pragmatic solution, the explanation for why the negative reason existential initially seems true must be the reason's low weight. But I think there is a better explanation. It's not that we ignore the reason because it's so weak; rather, I think that we simply *miss* the reason because it's so non-obvious. Now, I agree that, even once we acknowledge it, we'd do better to ignore it, since it's so lightweight. But the point is that the weight of the reason is not the explanation for why the negative reason existential sounds true. The amount of iron you could get from eating your car is simply not something we would ever think about, unless someone pointed it out to us. Confirmation for this explanation over Schroeder's comes from the fact that the difference in acceptability between (9) and (11) is more striking than the difference between (9) and (10):

(9) There's a reason to eat your car.
(10) There's a reason to eat your car, but it's a really weak one.
(11) The fact that it contains your daily recommended amount of iron is a reason to eat your car.

If Schroeder's explanation were correct, we should expect a much stronger difference between (9) and (10) than between (9) and (11), since (10) *explicitly* cancels the implicature that supposedly makes (9) sound false. But on my non-obviousness explanation, we should expect a stronger difference between (9) and (11). I think the data here confirm my explanation over Schroeder's.[23]

---

[22] This is actually not straightforward, since it would seem to require the following kind of assumption: if asserting $p$ in a context would have a false implicature, then asserting $\neg p$ in that context will sound true. This assumption is questionable.

[23] I agree that 'The fact that it contains your daily recommended amount of iron is a reason to eat your car, but it's a really weak one' sounds (a bit) better than (11). But I can explain that by pointing out that this claim is simply more informative than (11).

The important point for the Tom Grabit case is that the supposed reason, that you saw someone who looked just like Tom run out of the library with the book, isn't at all non-obvious. So we need a different explanation for the Tom Grabit case. I'll argue now that contrastivism offers an attractive explanation. The contrastivist explanation is also attractive because it holds that the intuitively true negative reason existential—Tom's complaint that we have no reason to think that he stole the book—is actually true, rather than trying to explain away that intuition.

### 2.5.3 A contrastivist solution

The puzzling data about negative reason existentials are that there are some claims like 'There is no reason to A' that are intuitively true, though we seem committed to there actually being reasons to A. Thinking about THE TWIN BOOK THIEF, 'There is no reason to believe that Tom stole the book' seems true. But when we consider THE TRIPLET BOOK THIEF, it seems that there is even *less* reason to believe that Tom stole the book in this case than in the previous one. So there couldn't have been *no* reason before, contrary to our intuitions about the negative reason existential. Once we reflect on this fact, we seem to be committed to the claim that there *is* a reason to believe that Tom stole the book in THE TWIN BOOK THIEF, after all.

Here's how to explain this phenomenon using contrastive reasons. In the context given by the THE TWIN BOOK THIEF, the most natural contrast to believing that Tom stole the book is believing that Tim, Tom's twin brother, stole the book, since this alternative has just been made relevant. And it's true that there is no reason to believe that Tom stole the book rather than believe that Tim stole the book. This is why it's true to say 'There's no reason to believe that Tom stole the book', when we're considering THE TWIN BOOK THIEF. But when we consider THE TRIPLET BOOK THIEF, and notice that there's even less reason to believe that Tom stole the book in this case than in the previous case, and so want to accept 'There is a reason to believe that Tom stole the book', the contrast to believing that Tom stole the book is most plausibly *not* believing (that is, failing to believe) that Tom stole the book.

Here's why. We need some reason that exists in both THE TWIN BOOK THIEF and in THE TRIPLET BOOK THIEF, whose weight we can compare across the cases. Since Tam wasn't in the picture in THE TWIN BOOK THIEF, we can't have in mind any reasons involving Tam. So the only two plausible candidates, on a contrastive framework, are a reason to believe that Tom stole the book rather than believing that Tim stole it and a reason to believe that Tom stole the book rather than not believing that Tom stole it. But there's no reason to believe that Tom stole the book rather than believing that Tim stole it in *either* case. So that leaves only a reason to believe that Tom stole it rather than not believing that Tom stole it. And there very plausibly is this reason in both cases, and it's very plausibly weaker in THE TRIPLET BOOK THIEF than it is in THE TWIN BOOK THIEF.

Any theory of reasons has to allow that some reasons are weightier than others, and that some consideration might be a weightier reason for one thing than it is for another thing. Contrastivism is no different—in THE TWIN BOOK THIEF, the fact that you saw (what looked like) Tom running out is a weightier reason to believe that he stole the book out of {believe that Tom stole the book, don't believe that Tom stole the book} than it is in THE TRIPLET BOOK THIEF.[24] This solution is available to the contrastivist because she holds that reasons are relativized to possibly non-exhaustive sets of alternatives. One fact can fail to be a reason to believe that *p* relative to one set, be a reason to believe that *p* relative to a second set, and be an even weightier reason to believe that *p* relative to a third set.

Contrastivism has a plausible explanation of why the negative reason existential is literally true, as well as why the positive reason existential that we accept after considering the comparative claim about the weight of reasons is true. The reason we're saying does not exist is a reason to believe that Tom stole the book out of {believe that Tom stole the book, believe that Tim stole the book}, while the reason whose weight we're comparing across cases is a reason to believe Tom stole the book out of {believe Tom stole the book, don't believe Tom stole the book}.[25] On a

---

[24] One important thing to keep in mind here is that, according to contrastivism, the weight of a reason to A out of Q does not depend on the weight of any non-contrastive reasons to A and non-contrastive reasons for the other alternatives in Q. That's because, of course, there just are no non-contrastive reasons. This does raise the question of how best to think about the weight of a contrastive reason, but virtually any theory needs to give some account of weight, and few do. I'll rely on an intuitive understanding.

[25] Some people deny that the negative reason existential even seems true. I think that framing things as I have done, by imagining Tom protesting when we accuse him of stealing the book, makes it even more intuitive that the claim is true. My hypothesis for their resistance is that they have in mind the set {believe that Tom stole the book, don't believe that Tom stole the book}. And contrastivism predicts that, relative to this set, there is a reason to believe that Tom stole the book, so the negative reason existential *should* seem false.

non-contrastive theory, on the other hand, these claims are incompatible. So this is an advantage for contrastivism: we need not bite the bullet and admit that one of our intuitive judgments is false. And moreover, contrastivism is independently well motivated by the puzzle about 'rather than' ascriptions.

## 2.6 Looking Forward

I've argued in this chapter that contrastivism about reasons gains some support from consideration of our talk about reasons. The solutions to the puzzles depend on the contrastive semantics that fit very naturally with contrastivism. But in the next chapter, I'll consider how far the argument in this chapter actually takes us.

# 3
# Favoring

In the previous chapter, I argued that certain features of our talk about reasons support contrastivism. Relativizing reason ascriptions to sets of alternatives solves puzzles that face non-contrastive theories. In this chapter, though, I'll consider how far that argument actually takes us. The puzzles concerned reason *ascriptions*, and the solutions came from a contrastive account of those ascriptions. It's very natural to think that this is strong support for the thesis that reasons are fundamentally contrastive. If reason ascriptions are contrast-sensitive, then it seems obvious that the reason relation, which presumably serves as the semantic content of 'reason', must be contrastive as well. But this is an apparently radical thesis, given that reasons are traditionally taken to be reasons for things *simpliciter*. We might hope, then, to avoid committing ourselves to this sort of theory prematurely.

## 3.1 Why Resist Contrastivism?

As I've emphasized, reasons are traditionally taken to be reasons for things *simpliciter*, independently of the contextually relevant alternatives. So the first reason why we might want to resist contrastivism is simply that it's *radical*. Nearly everyone who writes about reasons seems to assume a non-contrastive picture (usually implicitly, of course). So adopting contrastivism would require rejecting—or at least seriously reinterpreting—these writers' claims.

Second, contrastivism might seem mysterious. Scanlon (1998) says that reasons are considerations that count in favor of the things they are reasons for, and many other writers adopt this gloss. But, if we accept this gloss, contrastivism might seem puzzling: how could the relevant set of alternatives matter for whether or not some consideration counts in favor of an action or attitude, at a fundamental level? The *availability* of some alternative can arguably alter whether or not some consideration is a reason to do something. But contrastivism makes a more surprising claim than this, as I emphasized in Chapter 1. Reasons are reasons only *relative to* some set of alternatives, whether or not that set includes all of the available alternatives. So it's not simply the other available alternatives that matter in determining whether some consideration is a reason for an action: it also matters what we're comparing the action to. It is perhaps not terribly surprising that the relevant alternatives could make a difference in our interpretation of natural language reason ascriptions; it would be much more surprising if they could make a real normative difference.

Third, many theories in ethics and epistemology appeal to normative reasons, and some have even taken the notion of a reason to be *the* fundamental normative notion, reducing all other normative concepts to reasons.[1] But, if we complicate the fundamental normative relation by adding an argument place for a set of alternatives, we might worry that this will complicate our analyses of other normative concepts. Even if, as I argued in Chapter 1, contrastivism about reasons doesn't require us to be contrastivists about these other concepts, the analyses of these other concepts might be more complicated if we adopt contrastivism about reasons.

## 3.2 Shallow Contrastivism

The arguments for contrastivism in Chapter 2 concerned reason ascriptions. So, if we want to avoid contrastivism in the face of those arguments, a natural strategy is to develop a theory that can mimic the contrastivist's solution to the puzzles I presented in the previous chapter, while retaining a more traditional non-contrastive metaphysics to avoid some of the complications I mentioned in the previous section. To do this, we need a theory that offers a contrastive account of reason ascriptions but accepts a non-contrastive metaphysics of the important normative favoring relation that philosophers are concerned with when they theorize about reasons, and in terms of which we may want to analyze other important normative concepts. Call this kind of theory *shallow contrastivism*; call the more radical theory *deep contrastivism*.

---

[1] See, e.g., Scanlon (1998), Raz (1999), Schroeder (2007). See e.g., Broome (2004), and Väyrynen (2010) for skepticism about this project.

The basic shallow contrastivist idea is simple. Rather than tracking when some consideration does or does not favor an action *simpliciter*, our reason ascriptions track *the degree to which* the consideration favors the action as compared to the degree to which it favors the other relevant alternatives. So at the bottom we have a non-contrastive favoring relation: facts favor certain actions (or attitudes) to a certain degree *simpliciter*. When a fact *r* favors *A*-ing *more* than it favors *B*-ing, we can truly say '*r* is a reason to *A* rather than *B*'. Or, if *B*-ing is the contextually relevant alternative to *A*-ing, we can simply say '*r* is a reason to *A*', though what this means is that *r* favors *A*-ing more than it favors the contextually relevant alternatives.

This resembles a view I considered in the previous chapter, according to which reason ascriptions like '*r* is a reason to *A* rather than *B*' mean that *r* is a *stronger* reason to *A* than it is to *B*. I raised a couple of problems for that view, including the fact that it relies on an ad hoc treatment of 'rather than' in reason ascriptions. In other uses, 'rather than' does not mean anything like 'stronger than', but rather introduces alternatives. But importantly, the shallow contrastivist theory under consideration now does not face this problem. That's because this theory accepts the contrastive account of reason ascriptions I developed in the previous chapter. So we do not translate 'rather than' as 'stronger than'; rather, the 'rather than' clause just makes explicit the alternatives, just as it does in other uses. The notion of comparative strength, on this picture, applies to the *favoring* relation, which is appealed to in the analysis of what it is for some consideration to be a reason to *A* relative to some alternatives, not in the semantics of the reason ascriptions themselves. I'll have more to say about the relationship between the favoring relation and reason ascriptions shortly.

This view arguably has some precedent in Alastair Norcross's work defending consequentialism.[2] He says: "Our (moral) reasons for choosing between alternative actions, institutions, etc. are essentially comparative, and correspond to the comparative consequential value of the options." This quotation suggests that Norcross is actually a *deep* contrastivist about (moral) reasons. But he also says, in the next sentence: "I might have a better reason for choosing to do A than to do B, and better by a certain

---

[2] See Norcross (1997, 2005a, b).

amount, but neither reason is either good or bad *simpliciter*."[3] This quotation seems to fit better with a shallow contrastivist view, on which considerations favor alternatives with a certain weight, though we can call them (good or bad) reasons only relative to some comparison class. Moreover, Norcross understands his project as providing a contextualist *linguistic* theory for consequentialism, where context provides some appropriate alternatives, and we can say something is good or bad only *as compared* to these alternatives. But, at bottom, he seems to assume a traditional view of favoring.

Now I'll develop shallow contrastivism in more detail. First I'll outline a traditional non-contrastive account of the favoring relation, then I'll develop a contrastive account of reason claims and pair the two to end up with shallow contrastivism.

### 3.2.1 A traditional theory of favoring

A traditional, non-contrastive view of reasons says that reasons are considerations that favor certain actions with a certain weight or strength, some weightier than others. Most people agree that it's a mistake to identify the weight of a reason with a number, but for simplicity that's what I'll do here (or at least *represent* it as a number). So we can think of the relation that a fact stands in to the thing it favors as something like this: $F(r, A, x)$. This means that fact $r$ *favors* action $A$ with weight $x$. This is a relation that holds between facts, actions, and weights independently of contextually relevant alternatives. We can use this relation to obtain a *ranking* of alternatives based on how strongly $r$ favors them. So, if we have $F(r, A, 2)$ and $F(r, B, 5)$, we would rank $B$ above $A$ on the ranking of alternatives generated by $r$.[4] We can understand disfavoring as favoring with a *negative* weight: $F(r, A, -5)$, for example.[5] This favoring relation, according to shallow contrastivism, is the important normative relation that writers who talk about reasons are really concerned with, and the

---

[3] Norcross (2005a: 81).

[4] We can take more facts into consideration to obtain a ranking of how strongly all of the relevant considerations favor the different alternatives by performing some function on the weights with which each fact favors the various alternatives. (This is essentially the picture I sketched in Chapter 1 to show that contrastivism about 'ought' does not require contrastivism about reasons.)

[5] There might be complications here, but since I don't ultimately want to defend shallow contrastivism, I won't focus on those here.

relation in terms of which we may want to try to analyze other normative concepts. This would explain why nearly everyone glosses a reason as a consideration that *favors* some action or attitude (with a certain weight).

### 3.2.2 A contrastive account of reason claims

The next step is to pair this idea with a contrastive account of reason claims. I solved the puzzles about reason claims in the previous chapter by making bare reason claims context-sensitive: as the contextually relevant set of alternatives varies, the content of the reason ascription shifts. The shallow contrastivist can essentially just adopt this account of reason claims.

There's an apparent tension here. The account of reason ascriptions requires that the relation that serves as the semantic value of those ascriptions include an argument place for sets of alternatives, so that it can vary with them. But the shallow contrastivist wants the important normative favoring relation not to vary with the alternatives.

So what we have to do is reject the natural idea that instances of the underlying favoring relation are the semantic content of reason ascriptions. Instead, we need to posit an intermediate relation, $R(r, A, Q)$, to serve as the semantic content of reason ascriptions. $Q$ is the relevant set of alternatives. I'll call $R$ the 'reason relation', since it's the content of reason ascriptions. But all this means is that the fundamental relation—the one we really care about in ethics, epistemology, and so on—is not (what I'm calling) the reason relation, but is rather the favoring relation $F$.

We can ensure that the favoring relation $F$ is the more fundamental relation by analyzing $R$ in terms of $F$ in the following way:

**Shallow Reasons:** $R(r, A, Q)$ iff there's some $x$ such that $F(r, A, x)$, and for all $B$ in $Q$ not identical to $A$ there's some $y$ such that (i) $F(r, B, y)$, and (ii) $x > y$.

Intuitively what this says is that $r$ is a reason for $A$ out of $Q$ iff $r$ favors $A$ more than it favors any other alternative in $Q$. And then we say that '$r$ is a reason for $A$' is true in context $c$ iff $R(r, A, Q)$, for the relevant set of alternatives $Q$ in $c$.[6]

---

[6] There's one complication I want to address here. Some considerations intuitively don't stand in the favoring relation to some actions—not even with a negative weight. For example, the fact that $2 + 2 = 4$ doesn't seem to favor or disfavor my drinking another cup

So when philosophers say things like 'Reasons are considerations that count in favor of actions or attitudes', we have to do some mild reinterpretation: they mean that reasons are considerations that favor things *more* than they favor the relevant alternatives. This is not a very radical reinterpretation. When I say that $r$ is a reason to $A$, this can still be relevant for determining what I'm justified in doing, or what I ought to do. That's because my claim can be true only if $r$ really does favor (non-contrastively) $A$-ing, and does so more than it favors other relevant actions. And our analyses of concepts like 'ought' should technically proceed in terms of favoring, not reasons. So, instead of saying, for example, that you ought to $A$ when you have most reason to $A$, we can say that you ought to $A$ when $A$-ing is the most favored thing you can do.[7]

Shallow contrastivism can essentially adopt the semantic principles I gave in Chapter 2, but state things in terms of the $R$ relation, which can then be cashed out in terms of the underlying $F$ relation. Nothing about the solutions to the puzzles about reason claims depended on the relation that serves as the content of reason ascriptions being the fundamental relation. So the fact that deep contrastivism can solve puzzles is not (for all I've said so far) evidence for deep contrastivism over shallow contrastivism.

### 3.2.3 Shallow contrastivism and exclusivity

Before I evaluate shallow contrastivism, I want to point out one interesting commitment of shallow contrastivism. It requires that **Exclusivity** is

of coffee: there's no weight $x$ such that $F(2 + 2 = 4$, drink another cup of coffee, $x)$. One initially attractive idea is to say that, in these cases, the fact favors the action with weight zero. But this will give us odd results in some cases. Suppose that $r$ neither favors nor disfavors $A$, and slightly disfavors $B$. Then it would be true, on the theory as I've developed it so far, to say '$r$ is a reason to $A$', in a context in which the set of alternatives is $\{A, B\}$, since zero is greater than whatever negative number we use for the weight with which $r$ disfavors $B$. But it's strange to say that $r$ is a reason for $A$ when it's completely irrelevant to $A$. I think there are a couple of ways to respond to this problem. We could say instead that when $r$ is irrelevant to $A$, $r$ just doesn't stand in the $F$ relation to $A$ at all. Then it wouldn't be true to say that $r$ is a reason to $A$. A second solution is to bite the bullet and admit that, if the salient set of alternatives is $\{A, B\}$, and $r$ disfavors $B$, then it *is* a reason to $A$ *rather than B*. I don't think this is terribly implausible. For now, though, I'll just leave this issue aside.

[7] The particular analysis doesn't really matter. The one I've mentioned allows us to avoid contrastivism about 'ought', since $A$-ing has to be more favored than anything else you could do, not just more than some (potentially non-exhaustive) set of alternatives. A contrastive view of 'ought' (see Sloman 1970, Jackson 1985, Finlay 2009, Cariani 2009, 2013, Snedegar 2012) could say instead that you ought to $A$ when $A$-ing is more favored than any of the relevant alternatives.

true, at least in cases in which the relevant set of alternatives is $\{A, \neg A\}$. Here again is that principle:

> **Exclusivity:** If $r$ is a reason for $s$ to $A$, then $r$ is not also a reason for $s$ not to $A$.

Lots of people think that **Exclusivity** is true, so they won't see this as a problem for shallow contrastivism. But I gave a case in the previous chapter that I think is plausibly a counterexample to this principle.[8] The fact that the person across the bar is famous is a reason to talk to her, since I love to talk to famous people. But it's also a reason not to talk to her, since I hate to be snubbed, and famous people are likely to snub guys like me. If this case, or one like it, is a counterexample to **Exclusivity**, then shallow contrastivism has a problem.

Here's why. In the case I presented, the set of relevant alternatives is clearly {talk to her, don't talk to her}. For the fact that she's famous to be a reason to talk to her out of this set, according to the shallow contrastivist, this fact has to favor talking to her more than it favors not talking to her. And for it to be a reason not to talk to her out of this set, it has to favor not talking to her more than it favors talking to her. But this is impossible. If the shallow contrastivist's favoring relation is going to be anything like the traditional understanding of the favoring relation, then at least this much has to hold: if $r$ favors $A$-ing more than $B$-ing, then it doesn't also favor $B$-ing more than $A$-ing. So again, if **Exclusivity** is false, then shallow contrastivism is in trouble.[9] But, since lots of people accept **Exclusivity**, I won't put much weight on this. Instead, I'll now argue directly that the favoring relation itself is contrastive.

## 3.3 Favoring

In this section I'll assess the shallow contrastivist strategy for resisting deep contrastivism by discussing the favoring relation directly, rather than the reason relation. Most people, including deep contrastivists, will think these are just the same relation, of course. But this is exactly what

---

[8] See Dancy (1993: 62) for another.
[9] The deep contrastivist doesn't have this problem. The fact that she is famous is a reason to talk to her out of this set, and a reason not to talk to her out of this same set. But, since the explanations for these two reasons are different, we don't have a violation of **Restricted Exclusivity**.

the shallow contrastivist has to deny. The reason relation—the content of reason ascriptions—is contrastive. But this relation is analyzed in terms of the non-contrastive favoring relation; so, clearly, these relations must be distinct. I'll argue that the favoring relation itself is contrastive—facts favor actions or attitudes only relative to sets of alternatives.[10]

If the favoring relation is contrastive, that's strong support for deep contrastivism. First, the claim that reasons are considerations that favor things is ubiquitous. If considerations favor only things relative to sets of alternatives, it follows from this claim that they're only reasons relative to sets of alternatives. Second, and particularly relevant for this chapter, of course, is that if the favoring relation is contrastive, then shallow contrastivism is false. We can't resist deep contrastivism by appealing to a non-contrastive favoring relation.

### 3.3.1 Against non-contrastive favoring

The argument that favoring is always favoring relative to some set of alternatives, rather than favoring *simpliciter*, begins from the following case, adapted from Ross (2006). Suppose I have three dinner invitations, and that I must select exactly one: Invitation A is for Armenian with Ara. Invitation B is for burgers with Burt. Invitation C is for Chinese with Charlie. I love spending time with Ara, really like spending time with Burt, but can barely tolerate spending time with Charlie. On the other hand, I love Chinese, really like burgers, but can barely stomach Armenian.

The following claims are clearly true. The fact that Invitation B is for dinner with Burt favors choosing Invitation B rather than choosing Invitation C. And the fact that Invitation B is for burgers favors choosing Invitation B rather than choosing Invitation A. But does the fact that Invitation B is for dinner with Burt favor choosing Invitation B *simpliciter*? Or does the fact that Invitation B is for burgers favor choosing Invitation B *simpliciter*? It might seem like the answer to both questions is clearly 'yes': after all, these two facts favor choosing Invitation B rather than

---

[10] The argument I'll give is a development of a discussion in Ross (2006: ch. 9). I should note that Ross is careful to keep contrastivism about reasons at arm's length, claiming merely that talking in terms of contrastive reasons and contrastive favoring avoids some difficulties—difficulties that I'll develop into full-fledged objections—and is thus more convenient for his purposes.

Invitations C and A, respectively. And, given that we are talking about a non-contrastive favoring relation, how could they do that if they didn't favor choosing Invitation B *simpliciter*?

But the following claims are also true. The fact that Invitation B is for dinner with Burt does not favor choosing Invitation B rather than Invitation A—after all, I like spending time with Ara more than I like spending time with Burt. And, similarly, the fact that Invitation B is for burgers does not favor choosing Invitation B rather than Invitation C— after all, I like Chinese food more than I like burgers. So perhaps these facts actually don't favor choosing Invitation B *simpliciter*. I could do better with respect to my food preferences by not choosing Invitation B, and I could do better with respect to my dinner companion preferences by not choosing Invitation B.

But, given the set-up of the case, it's very plausible—or should at least be possible—that, all things considered, I ought to choose Invitation B. If neither of the relevant facts—that Invitation B is for burgers, and that it's for dinner with Burt—favors choosing B, then it looks like *nothing* favors choosing Invitation B. But now we have an odd result: I ought to choose Invitation B, though nothing favors choosing it. So it seems implausible, if you're a non-contrastivist about favoring, to say that these facts don't favor choosing Invitation B *simpliciter*. But, as we have just seen, there are difficulties with saying that these facts do favor choosing Invitation B *simpliciter*, as well. In particular, they do not favor choosing Invitation B rather than Invitations A and C, respectively.

At this point, we can conclude (with Ross, 2006) the following. There are cases, like the one above, in which it's very hard to say whether some fact favors some action *simpliciter*, but very easy to say whether it favors the action *rather than* some other action. My suggestion is that this is because the favoring relation is fundamentally contrastive. Cases like this one make this clear: to answer the question 'Does r favor A-ing?', we have to know 'Rather than what?'. In lots of cases that philosophers have been interested in, the relevant consideration favors the relevant action rather than any of the salient alternatives, so it's not so important to specify the alternatives. But in cases like this one, it *is* important.

This argument looks a lot like one I gave in Chapter 2 to argue for the contrastive account of reason ascriptions. The shallow contrastivist's response was to accept that argument, but posit a more fundamental non-contrastive favoring relation. So one possible move here is to adopt a contrastive account of 'favoring' ascriptions, and posit an even more fundamental non-contrastive proto-favoring relation. But this strategy will lead nowhere, except to more cases like this one that call into question the non-contrastivity of the proto-favoring relation.

A different strategy is just to stick with the favoring relation, and appeal to the fact that favoring comes in degrees. This is very similar to the response involving RT-1 in the previous chapter, which held that $r$ is a reason for $A$ rather than $B$ when $r$ is a better reason for $A$ than it is for $B$. I rejected this strategy because it gives an ad hoc treatment of 'rather than' in reason ascriptions. So this response will face that same problem. But, after spelling out this idea, I will argue that, even if we set that problem aside, there is a more serious difficulty.

So, first, here is the response. We should understand 'rather than' favoring claims as simple comparisons of how much the consideration favors each of the actions. So when I said that the fact that Invitation B is for burgers favors choosing it rather than Invitation A, that was true. But what this means is just that this fact favors choosing Invitation B *more* than it favors choosing Invitation A; we don't need a fundamentally contrastive favoring relation to explain this.

I think this response is problematic. I will first raise a problem for this simple version of the response and then consider more sophisticated versions; I will argue that these also fail.

So first, here's the argument against the simple version of the response. The fact that Invitation B is for burgers does not favor choosing Invitation B rather than Invitation C—remember that I like Chinese food more than burgers. According to the response being considered, this means that the fact that Invitation B is for burgers does not favor choosing it more than it favors choosing Invitation C. But this fact doesn't seem to favor choosing Invitation C at all—it doesn't have anything to do with Invitation C. So, if we insist that it does favor choosing Invitation B *simpliciter*, we have to say that, despite this, it does not favor choosing Invitation B more than it favors choosing Invitation C, even though it doesn't favor choosing Invitation C *at all*. This is hard to make sense of.

Here's a more sophisticated version of this response. Perhaps I've actually misidentified the relevant facts that do the favoring in this case. The relevant facts are the following two more complicated facts:

(i) Invitation A is for Armenian and Invitation B is for burgers and Invitation C is for Chinese.

(ii) Invitation A is for dinner with Ara and Invitation B is for dinner with Burt and Invitation C is for dinner with Charlie.

Fact (i) favors choosing Invitation C to the highest degree, choosing B to a slightly lower degree, and choosing A to a much lower degree. Fact (ii) favors choosing Invitation A to the highest degree, choosing B to a slightly lower degree, and choosing C to a much lower degree. As suggested above, 'rather than' claims simply give us comparisons between the degree to which the relevant fact favors the options. The reason why I ought to choose Invitation B, all things considered, is that it is the most favored option, once we add up the amounts provided by facts (i) and (ii).

This view does seem to avoid the problems I've presented so far, but it has the counterintuitive consequence that, *strictly speaking*, the fact that Invitation B is for burgers *doesn't* favor choosing it rather than Invitation A. It's only the more complicated fact (i) that favors choosing Invitation B rather than Invitation A. A contrastive theory of favoring doesn't have this consequence. We can avoid saying that our ordinary claims and intuitions about what favors what are actually false, or at least incomplete. The facts about the other invitations that are built into (i) and (ii) can serve as what Schroeder calls *background conditions*, or what Dancy calls *enablers*.[11] They are part of what makes it the case that the simpler facts favor the relevant alternative, but need not themselves be part of the favorer.

In fact there is good reason to think that this is the right way to think about these other facts. In discussing background conditions, Schroeder introduces a very plausible *Deliberative Constraint*: when you deliberate, what you should be thinking about are the things that count in favor of or against the alternatives. Now suppose that what really count in favor of the alternatives in this case are the complicated facts (i) and (ii). And suppose that, for whatever reason, I am ignoring Invitation C, and deliberating only between Invitations A and B. According to the Deliberative Constraint, I should still be thinking about facts (i) and (ii), which include considerations about Invitation C. But it is bizarre to think that I have to think about considerations involving Invitation C when I am just deliberating between Invitations A and B. So, as long as we accept the

---

[11] See Dancy (2004: ch. 3); Schroeder (2007: ch. 2).

Deliberative Constraint, we should think that what does the favoring are the simpler facts. For example, what favors Invitation B is the fact that Invitation B is for burgers, and the fact that Invitation B is for dinner with Burt.

So assume that what does the favoring are these simpler facts. I have argued that the problem with the simple 'rather than' as 'more than' idea is that, though it can explain why the fact that Invitation B is for burgers favors choosing B rather than choosing A, it cannot explain why this fact does not favor choosing B rather than choosing C. For this response to explain this, it would have to be that, though the fact that B is for burgers favors choosing B to some degree, it does not favor choosing B more than it favors choosing C, even though it has nothing whatsoever to do with C, and so doesn't seem to favor C at all.

Here is one reasonable reaction to this argument. It is true that the fact that Invitation B is for burgers doesn't favor Invitation C at all—it just doesn't have anything to do with Invitation C. But, for that very reason, it sounds odd to compare the degree to which it favors B with the degree to which it favors C in the first place. In fact, Invitations A and C are on a par here—the fact that Invitation B is for burgers also has nothing to do with Invitation A. So it is odd to compare the degree to which this fact favors choosing Invitation B with the degree to which it favors choosing Invitation A, as well. If that's right, then this strategy cannot even explain why the fact that Invitation B is for burgers favors choosing Invitation B rather than choosing Invitation A. This suggests that this was just not the right kind of strategy in the first place.

Here is a different strategy.[12] Instead of focusing on whether the fact itself favors one thing more than another, we look at the objective that explains why the fact favors the action.[13] For example, the fact that Invitation B is for burgers favors choosing Invitation B because of the objective of getting a delicious meal. When an objective $O$ explains why $r$ favors $A$-ing, say that $r$ $O$-favors $A$-ing. So consider the following claim:

**O-Favoring:** $r$ favors $A$ rather than $B$ iff $r$ $O$-favors $A$ more than any fact $O$-favors $B$.

---

[12] This was suggested to me by Joe Nelson.

[13] I introduced this idea, about objectives providing reasons, in the previous chapter. I will have much more to say about it in the next chapter.

Since I really like burgers, the fact that Invitation B is for burgers *delicious meal*-favors choosing Invitation B to some degree. Given that I don't like Armenian food, there is no fact that *delicious meal*-favors choosing Invitation A to a higher degree. Thus, the fact that Invitation B is for burgers favors choosing B rather than choosing A. On the other hand, there is a fact that *delicious meal*-favors choosing C to a higher degree than the degree to which the fact that Invitation B is for burgers *delicious meal*-favors choosing B. This is the fact that Invitation C is for Chinese food. Thus, the fact that Invitation B is for burgers does not favor choosing B rather than choosing C, according to **O-Favoring**. This is the result we wanted.

Besides delivering the right results in this case, I think this strategy also seems quite natural. If we ask why the fact that Invitation B is for burgers does not favor choosing B rather than choosing C, an explanation in terms of the objective of getting a delicious meal does seem apt. As we will see in the next chapter, my contrastive theory of reasons bears certain similarities to this picture. Both make central use of the objectives involved in explaining why some fact favors, or is a reason for, one alternative rather than another. But, as I will now argue, this picture faces a problem; the view I develop in the next chapter avoids this problem.

The problem with this strategy is that **O-Favoring** (as well as the simpler 'more than' analysis of 'rather than' favoring ascriptions I have considered) validates the following inference:

**Favoring RT:** If *r* favors *A* rather than *B*, then *r* favors *A*.

If *r* O-favors *A* more than anything O-favors *B*, then *r* O-favors *A* to some degree. And this just means that *r* favors *A*, and this favoring is explained by objective *O*. Note that this is just the favoring version of the principle about reasons, RT, that I discussed in the previous chapter. This principle was the source of the non-contrastivist's trouble with 'rather than' reason ascriptions, as illustrated by the jog–bike–drive to campus case.

So consider that case, but this time stated in terms of favoring. The fact that campus is twenty miles away favors biking rather than jogging. The objective that explains this is my desire not to wear myself out getting to campus. So, according to **O-Favoring**, since it validates **Favoring RT**, the fact that campus is twenty miles away favors biking. But it is also obvious in this case that the fact that campus is twenty miles away favors not biking—after all, I could just drive instead. (The claim is not that

O-Favoring entails this; the claim is that this is just obviously true in this case.) And this favoring fact is also explained by my desire not to wear myself out getting to campus. So we have a violation of the favoring version of **Restricted Exclusivity**, which states that no single fact can both favor A and favor not-A, where both instances of favoring are explained by the same objective.

The defender of a fundamentally non-contrastive favoring relation (the shallow contrastivist, for example) could offer a more complicated story about these 'rather than' favoring claims. But I do think I've said enough to show that whatever the non-contrastivist says about favoring is going to have to be somewhat complicated, or have some counterintuitive consequences. The contrastivist, on the other hand, offers a neat explanation. The fact that Invitation B is for burgers favors choosing Invitation B out of {choose Invitation B, choose Invitation A}, but not out of {choose Invitation B, choose Invitation C}. There's just no question about whether some consideration favors choosing Invitation B *simpliciter*, since all favoring is favoring out of a set of alternatives.

## 3.4 Contrastive Reasons and Favoring

So far, in describing contrastivism, I've remained at a pretty abstract level. In this section, I'll develop contrastivism further. In particular, I will consider the relationship between contrastive reasons and what an agent ought to do. To lead into this discussion, I'll first raise a problem for contrastivism about the favoring relation.

### 3.4.1 Contrastivism

Here is the contrastivist version of the idea that reasons are considerations that favor the things they are reasons for:

> **Contrastive Reasons:** A reason to A out of Q is a consideration that favors A-ing out of Q.

If we adopt **Contrastive Reasons**, we have two options. First, we can take the favoring relation, and so the reason relation, as primitive, like Scanlon (1998, 2014) and Parfit (2011). Second, we could try to give some analysis of this relation, saying what it takes for some consideration to be a reason for, or to favor, some alternative out of a set of alternatives. In this section, I'll just talk in terms of favoring, without offering an analysis. But in the next chapter I'll show that contrastivism fits nicely with a popular idea about how to analyze this relation, in terms of *promotion*.

### 3.4.2 A problem

I have shown that by adopting contrastivism about the favoring relation, which we can now just identify with the reason relation, we can make good sense of the dinner invitations case above. The fact that Invitation B is for burgers favors choosing it rather than choosing Invitation A, but does not favor choosing it rather than choosing Invitation C. And the fact that Invitation B is for dinner with Burt favors choosing it rather than choosing Invitation C, but does not favor choosing it rather than choosing Invitation A. These are exactly the claims we want to make about this case, and contrastivism lets us make them unproblematically.

So far, so good. But there is a problem. Which invitation should I choose? The relevant set is clearly {choose Invitation A, choose Invitation B, choose Invitation C}. And, given a natural specification of the case, I should choose Invitation B. But—just as it was hard to say whether anything favored choosing Invitation B *simpliciter*—it's not clear that anything favors choosing Invitation B relative to this set. After all, considerations about what I eat seem to favor choosing C relative to this set, while considerations about whom I eat with seem to favor choosing A relative to this set.

It isn't surprising that the same, or at least an analogous, issue should arise here, since I stipulated in this case that I have to choose exactly one of the three invitations. So the set {choose Invitation A, choose Invitation B, choose Invitation C} is, in this case, exhaustive. Contrastivism about favoring allows us to explain why the relevant considerations favor choosing Invitation B rather than Invitation A on the one hand, and rather than Invitation C on the other hand. But I haven't yet said anything to get around the problem of saying whether anything favors choosing Invitation B relative to the larger set.[14] To translate into the language of reasons the problem is that it does not look like either food considerations

---

[14] This problem actually depends on a certain understanding of what it takes for a fact to favor some action out of a set of alternatives. In the next chapter, I'll say more about this. For now, it's enough that intuitively, the fact that Invitation B is for burgers/dinner with Burt doesn't favor accepting Invitation B out of the larger set of alternatives, since I could both do better with respect to my food preferences by choosing one alternative, and do better with respect to my dinner company preferences by choosing a different alternative.

or companion considerations are reasons to choose Invitation B, out of the larger set of alternatives. Thus, it is hard to see how it could be true that I *ought* to accept Invitation B. To solve this problem, I need to say something about the relationship between an agent's reasons and what she ought to do.

### 3.4.3 Reasons and ought

The problem is that it's hard to see how we can say that I ought to accept Invitation B out of {accept Invitation A, accept Invitation B, accept Invitation C}, since it seems that neither the fact that Invitation B is for burgers nor the fact that it's for dinner with Burt is a reason to accept it out of this set. To solve this problem, I'm going to give a (somewhat) non-obvious account of the relationship between contrastive reasons and ought. But, after presenting this account, I will argue that, even though it may be non-obvious, it is on reflection quite natural.

Perhaps the most obvious way to understand the relationship between reasons and ought, for a contrastivist, is the following ('CRO' for 'Contrastive Reasons and Ought', '*' because I'm eventually going to reject it):

CRO*:   $s$ ought to $A$ out of $Q$ iff $s$ has most reason to $A$ out of $Q$.

Note that this principle appeals to a contrastive ought, as well as contrastive reasons. I argued in Chapter 1 that contrastivism about reasons neither requires nor is required by contrastivism about ought, but it's hard to deny that the two do fit together nicely. CRO* is the most obvious contrastivist principle, but it generates the problem I'm trying to solve. If neither the fact that Invitation B is for burgers nor the fact that it's for dinner with Burt is a reason to accept it out of the larger set, then it is hard to see how there could be *most* reason to accept Invitation B out of this set.

CRO* appeals to reasons out of arbitrarily large sets of alternatives—$Q$ can contain as many members as you like. But, as we've seen, it can be hard to say whether some fact is a reason out of larger sets of alternatives, though it's generally easy to say whether it's a reason out of two member sets.[15] So I propose to make use of the facts about what's a reason

---

[15] Of course, in many cases it's easy to say whether some fact is a reason out of a larger set: in most situations, the fact that I'm hungry is a reason to eat lunch out of {eat lunch, throw all my food in the garbage, run a mile, watch a movie} (assuming these are all mutually exclusive).

for what out of these two member sets in determining what an agent ought to do out of larger sets:

**CRO:** *s* ought to *A* out of *Q* iff *s* has most reason to *A* out of {*A*, *B*} for all of the other alternatives *B* in *Q*.

When *A* wins in all of the pairwise comparisons with other members in the set, you ought to *A*. CRO may be less obvious than CRO*, but it's not ad hoc. First, the action you ought to perform according to this principle is the *Condorcet winner*. The well-studied Condorcet method of voting is one in which a candidate wins an election when it wins in each pairwise comparison with the other candidates. Second, and more importantly, I think CRO is one plausible way for the contrastivist to capture the intuitive idea that you ought to *A* when *A*-ing is best *on balance*, even if it's not the best in any particular category. These are precisely the cases in which CRO* and CRO will come apart, and come apart in a way that favors CRO.

The dinner invitation case is this sort of case: Invitation B isn't best with respect to my food preferences, nor is it the best with respect to my dinner companion preferences. But it's best *on balance*, and that's why I ought to accept it. There's most reason to accept Invitation B out of {accept Invitation A, accept Invitation B} because, though I slightly prefer Ara's company to Burt's, I greatly prefer burgers to Armenian food.[16] Though the fact that Invitation A is for dinner with Ara is a reason to accept Invitation A out of this set, it's relatively weak, since I also really like to spend time with Burt (though not quite as much as I like to spend time with Ara). On the other hand, the fact that Invitation B is for burgers is a relatively strong reason to accept Invitation B out of this set. Similar reasoning shows that there's most reason to accept Invitation B out of {accept Invitation B, accept Invitation C}. Thus, according to CRO, I ought to accept Invitation B out of the larger set; this is the verdict we want.

CRO will be the principle I adopt going forward about the relationship between reasons and ought. This principle allows the contrastivist to avoid the problem I raised for the shallow contrastivist in the previous section.

---

[16] The idea here is that the strength of the reason corresponds in some way to the strength of the preference. I don't mean to endorse this as a perfectly general principle, but it does seem very plausible in cases like this one, assuming that my dinner companion preferences and my food preferences are of relatively equal importance.

It is worth reiterating something I said in Chapter 1: it is possible to hold that there is at least something very much like a non-contrastive ought—what you *really* ought to do—while still accepting contrastivism about reasons, and indeed accepting everything I've said so far in this chapter. To do this, we can adopt **CRO**, but hold that when we are trying to determine what you really ought to do, we need to look at a particular, privileged set of alternatives. For example, perhaps to determine whether you non-contrastively ought to A, we should look at {A, ¬A}, or perhaps we should look at the set of alternatives that includes every single option that's available to you, individuating alternatives at the finest level of detail at which you can intentionally determine that you perform one of them rather than the others. These options are available, but, when the question of what you ought to do comes up, I will generally not focus on these kinds of 'privileged' sets.

## 3.5 Looking Forward

In this chapter, I have introduced a distinction between shallow contrastivism and deep contrastivism. The arguments from reason claims in the previous chapter are neutral between these two versions. But I have argued that there's good reason to prefer deep contrastivism. This is because the shallow contrastivist has to appeal to a non-contrastive *favoring* relation, which underlies the contrastive reason relation, but the favoring relation itself is contrastive. I began to develop a contrastivist account of favoring, and so of reasons, but ran into trouble with the relationship between ought and reasons. To solve this problem, I have adopted a certain view about this relationship.

In the next chapter, I'll continue developing contrastivism. In particular, I'll show that the contrastivist can accommodate—and in fact is in a better position to capture—the widespread idea that reasons (and favoring) should be analyzed in terms of promotion. The account I'll develop there isn't a competitor to the account I have sketched in this chapter in terms of favoring. Instead, it's one way of further spelling out the view from this chapter by giving an analysis of the favoring relation. I'll also continue to investigate the depth of contrastivism, and argue for a somewhat moderate form of deep contrastivism.

# 4
# Promotion

In the previous chapter, I argued that the favoring relation, which people writing about reasons generally identify with the reason relation, is contrastive. This closes off the shallow contrastivist strategy for dealing with the puzzles about reason claims from Chapter 2. I also began to develop contrastivism about reasons. The view, as I've stated it so far, says that some fact is a reason to $A$ out of $Q$ when it favors $A$-ing out of $Q$. This is just the contrastivist implementation of the ubiquitous idea that reasons are considerations that count in favor of the things they're reasons for.

I motivated shallow contrastivism by raising some worries about how radical deep contrastivism is. Now that I've argued against shallow contrastivism, these worries are live once again. In the first section of this chapter, I'll make this concern especially sharp by introducing a problem for contrastivism. According to contrastivism, reasons for and against an option can vary with the alternatives—this is the central feature of contrastivism, and the one that lets us solve problems facing non-contrastive theories. But this variation cannot be totally *unconstrained*—knowing what reasons there are relative to one set should tell us *something* about the reasons relative to certain other sets. The problem facing the contrastivist is simply that she seems unable to provide these constraints.

The remainder of the chapter will be concerned with developing a detailed version of contrastivism that solves this problem. This will essentially involve spelling out the view I introduced in the previous chapter in terms of *promotion*. This taps into a widespread idea about how to analyze the reason relation. I'll argue that, in fact, this idea itself supports contrastivism: the best way to make good on the idea that reasons are tied to promotion is on a contrastive framework. This argument motivates a particular version of contrastivism that straightforwardly entails just the right kinds of constraints on the variation of reasons between different sets of alternatives.

## 4.1 The Need for Constraints

The contrastivist gains advantages over the traditional non-contrastive picture by making reasons relative to different sets of alternatives independent of one another. The problem that I will spell out in this section is that this independence needs to be *constrained* in certain ways, but the contrastivist seems to have no way to do this. Moreover, she must be careful in trying to solve this problem, so that she doesn't constrain the independence of reasons relative to different sets so much that she loses advantages over non-contrastive theories.

*4.1.1 Intransitivity*

Suppose I want to get in shape. Then the fact that physical exertion helps one get in shape is a reason to jog to the 101 Coffee Shop for my daily milkshake, rather than walk there. Similarly, it's a reason to walk there rather than drive. Is it a reason to jog rather than drive? Of course. And any plausible theory of what makes some consideration a reason for one thing rather than another will say so.

But the important thing to notice for my purposes here is that we shouldn't have to think about this at all—we shouldn't have to make an independent comparison of jogging and driving. Once we know it's a reason to jog rather than walk, and a reason to walk rather than drive, it should just *follow* that it's a reason to jog rather than drive. More generally, if $r$ is a reason for $A$ rather than $B$ and a reason for $B$ rather than $C$, it should simply follow that $r$ is a reason for $A$ rather than $C$. To deny this is to allow for a very troubling kind of intransitivity.[1]

The problem for the contrastivist is that nothing about the theory, for all that's been said, seems to rule out this kind of intransitivity. Since reasons relative to different sets are independent of one another—as they need to be for contrastivism to gain advantages over non-contrastive theories—we have no reason to think that the reason relation will guarantee that reasons for $A$ rather than $B$ and for $B$ rather than $C$ will be reasons for

---

[1] This isn't the same kind of intransitivity that receives a lot of attention in the literature, the intransitivity of 'better than' or 'more reason than'. See especially Temkin (1987, 2012), Rachels (1998, 2001), Friedman (2009) for advocates; see, e.g., Broome (1991) for defense of the much more common view that intransitivity is impossible. Nevertheless, the sort of intransitivity at issue here does seem problematic, as well. I will discuss the more common sort of intransitivity in the next chapter.

A rather than C. Ruling out this intransitivity is one important way in which the independence of reasons relative to different sets of alternatives should be constrained.

### 4.1.2 Reasons for and subsets

The fact that Bill has high blood pressure is a reason for him to order fish out of {order fish, order pork, order beef}.[2] If the waiter comes back to the table and tells Bill that the restaurant is out of pork, or ordering pork becomes irrelevant for some other reason, that obviously shouldn't change this: the fact that he has high blood pressure is still a reason to order fish out of {order fish, order beef}. And, again, any plausible theory about what makes a consideration a reason for an action out of a set of alternatives will say so.

But, again, the important point is that we shouldn't have to make an independent comparison of fish and beef. It should just follow that, in general, when $r$ is a reason for $A$ out of $\{A, B, C\}$, it's also a reason for $A$ out of $\{A, B\}$. Even more generally, reasons for an alternative out of one set should also be reasons for that alternative out of arbitrary subsets that include the alternative. If $r$ is a reason for $A$ when some other option $B$ is relevant, making $B$ irrelevant should not change this.

At this point, I want briefly to digress from the main thread to discuss an apparent counterexample to this entailment relation. I do so because seeing why it is not in fact a counterexample helps clarify the main contrastivist thesis by distinguishing it from a more widely held thesis. Suppose you want to pick the brightest color from a range of colors in front of you: A, B, and C. Owing to features of our visual system, in the presence of C, A appears brighter than B. But, if C is not present, A does not look brighter than B. Thus, it seems that your goal of picking the brightest color gives you a reason to choose A out of {choose A, choose B, choose C}, but does not give you a reason to choose A out of {choose A, choose B}.

To see why this is not in fact a counterexample to the entailment relation, we need to distinguish between the variability of reasons with the relevant alternatives, or with the contrasts, and the variability of reasons with the circumstances of choice. The circumstances of choice may include

---

[2] I'm assuming that these alternatives are mutually exclusive—Bill can order at most one of the dishes.

various things, but, for my purposes here, the most important things they include are features of the environment. In particular, in this example, the presence or absence of color C will be part of the circumstances. Many philosophers hold that the circumstances of choice can affect what reasons there are.[3] On the other hand, the central thesis of contrastivism is that reasons can vary not (only) with the circumstances, but (also) with the contrasts—the alternative actions we are comparing. The entailment relation, that reasons for $A$ out of $Q$ are also reasons for $A$ out of subsets of $Q$ that contain $A$, concerns shifts in the contrasts, not the circumstances. So the entailment holds only as long as we hold the circumstances fixed. Thus, we need to hold the presence or absence of color C fixed. If we assume that C is present, then color A will appear brighter than color B. So you will have a reason to choose A not only out of {choose A, choose B, choose C}, but also out of {choose A, choose B}—again, since C is present, A will look brighter than B. We have removed choosing C as a relevant alternative, but have not removed the presence of C as part of the circumstances. So the entailment relation survives this apparent counterexample.

### 4.1.3 Reasons against and supersets

Now suppose the fact that Bill has high blood pressure is a reason *against* ordering beef out of {order fish, order pork, order beef}. If the waiter comes back and informs Bill that the restaurant also has a salad, he shouldn't have to reconsider whether the fact that he has high blood pressure is a reason against ordering beef. Adding a new relevant alternative shouldn't change this. In general, reasons against an alternative out of one set are intuitively reasons against that alternative out of *supersets* of that set.

Apparent counterexamples to this constraint (which can be amended to target either of the other constraints I've discussed) involve cases in which learning about the new option gives the agent new information about the old options. So, for example, Bill may know that the restaurant serves salad only on nights when Chef Jack Sprat is working, and that Chef Sprat prepares beef in a heart-healthy way. Thus, upon learning that the restaurant is serving salad, it seems that the fact that he has high

---

[3] Dancy's holism (2004) about reasons is a particularly clear statement of this thesis, but, again, I think it is widely held.

blood pressure is not a reason against ordering the beef, since the beef is actually heart-healthy. I'll offer two replies. First, what has changed here is Bill's information; this may make it so that he no longer has a *subjective* reason, or a reason relative to his information, against ordering beef. But it is no surprise that Bill's subjective reasons can change with his information; the constraints are just meant to hold relative to the same body of information. But Bill's *objective* reasons have not changed—since Chef Sprat is in the kitchen, there was never actually any objective reason against ordering the beef (at least not one related to Bill's blood pressure). Second, if we don't like the distinction between objective and subjective reasons, we could simply adopt a more fine-grained view of the options: 'order beef when Chef Sprat makes it' is a different option from 'order beef when Chef Sprat's wife makes it', or 'order beef when salad is available' is different from 'order beef when salad is not available', or 'order heart-healthy beef' is different from 'order heart-unhealthy beef'.[4]

### 4.1.4 Entailment relations and deliberation

These and other intuitive entailment relations should hold between reasons relative to different but related sets.[5] I have motivated this thought by describing examples in which violation of these entailments seems very implausible. The more general idea, which these cases are meant to bring out, is the following. Reasons are used in deliberating about what to do— a central sort of deliberation involves weighing up reasons for and against various options. Often, this deliberation takes place over time, and as time passes, the salient alternatives can shift in various ways. Alternatives that were initially irrelevant may become relevant, or vice versa, for example. Since the contrastivist holds that reasons shift as the relevant alternatives shift, it seems that she is committed to saying that the reasons to be used in deliberation can shift. Thus, if the alternatives shift, it seems that the agent will have to abandon the results of her previous deliberation— those reasons aren't in play anymore. This would make cross-context deliberation impossible. But of course it is not impossible. What the cases I've described are meant to bring out is that there are *constraints* on how

---

[4] Thanks to Ephraim Glick and Don Hubin for calling my attention to these kinds of cases, which are common in the decision theory literature.
[5] I'll say more about entailments between sets that differ in resolution—how the alternatives are individuated—in Section 4.5.3.

the reasons can shift as the alternatives shift. Even if some of an agent's reasons shift as the relevant alternatives shift, others do not. This is the problem facing the contrastivist that I'll attempt to solve in the remainder of the chapter. To do so, though, I will first turn to a discussion of the relationship between reasons and the promotion of objectives. Closer to the end of the chapter, I will circle back to this problem and show how our account of reasons in terms of promotion straightforwardly provides the kinds of constraints we need.

## 4.2 Promotion

In this section, I'll argue that the popular idea that reasons are intimately related to the promotion of some kind of *objectives*—the satisfaction of desires, the realization of values, and so on—supports contrastivism. I mean for 'objectives' to be a technical term, standing for whatever it is that is to be promoted on these sorts of theories. I'll raise problems for non-contrastive views that contrastivism avoids; these problems do not necessarily prove conclusively that all non-contrastive theories are false, but they do provide independent support for the version of contrastivism I will develop.

### 4.2.1 Promotion in the theory of reasons

Several writers with importantly different views about the nature of normative reasons accept something like the following schema:

**Promote:** There is a reason for $s$ to $A$ iff $s$'s $A$-ing would promote some objective of the relevant kind.

Some writers, such as Moore (1903, 1912), Wedgwood (2009), and Parfit (2011), take the objectives to be values, like happiness or justice.[6] Others, like Schroeder (2007), take the relevant kind of objectives to be the objects of the desires of the agent. And others, like Finlay (2006, 2014), take the relevant kind of objective to be contextually specified ends. Nagel (1970) also analyzes reasons in terms of promotion, though his view is

---

[6] Moore talked about rightness rather than reasons, but his view of rightness would extend straightforwardly to this kind of view of reasons.

importantly different. Still, there is a plausible view in the neighborhood of Nagel's that fits **Promote**.[7]

Writers such as Scanlon (1998) and Anderson (1993) draw a distinction between promoting values and respecting or honoring values. If we make this distinction, we might worry that some reasons will not be explained by, or even involve, the promotion of anything. For example, according to this view, the value of friendship primarily gives us reasons to do things that would respect or honor friendships, say treating our friends well, rather than things that would promote friendship, say matching up people we think would make good friends.[8] The argument for contrastivism that I will give shortly is that the idea that reasons involve promotion is best captured on a contrastive theory. If not all reasons involve promotion, then this argument at best would seem to show that some reasons—those that involve promotion—are contrastive. But contrastivism, as I want to defend it, is the thesis that all reasons are contrastive.

I think we can allow that some reasons do not involve promotion, but rather involve respecting or honoring values, without limiting the scope of contrastivism in this way. Everyone should recognize that at least some reasons involve promotion. For example, instrumental reasons to take the means to our ends seem to be clearly tied to the promotion of those ends.[9] And, if I am right that these reasons are contrastive, that is some pressure to adopt contrastivism about all reasons. It is theoretically unattractive to posit two separate reason relations, one of which is contrastive and one of which is non-contrastive. If there is a plausible unified view of reasons on offer, that would be preferable.

I will develop my contrastive theory in terms of promotion, since (i) everyone should agree that some reasons involve promotion, and (ii) doing so will simplify exposition of the view. At the end of the chapter, however, I will return to this point and show how to extend the view to cover non-promotional reasons.

---

[7] The complication with Nagel's view is that he thinks what we have reasons to do is to promote valuable states of affairs, whereas the other theories hold that the fact that performing certain actions would promote certain objectives is what explains why we have reasons to do those actions. So, on Nagel's view, the concept of promotion shows up in what we have reason to do, while, on the other views, it shows up in the account of what it is for some fact to be a reason for us to perform some action.

[8] See Pettit (1991) and Pettit's contribution to Baron et al. (1997) for a defense of the view that all reasons involve promotion.

[9] See Bedke (2012), Kolodny (forthcoming) for relevant discussion.

Here is an important question at this point: what is it to promote an objective? One natural and popular answer is that your *A*-ing promotes an objective *O* when it raises the probability of *O*. Several authors have understood promotion in probabilistic terms.[10] So, for example, promoting the satisfaction of a desire is simply making it more probable that the desire is satisfied, promoting the realization of a value is making it more probable that the value is realized or instantiated, and so on. You may be wondering at this point, 'More probable *than what*?'. It will emerge shortly that I think this is a crucial question. Even so, though, this is a plausible, if not extremely informative, way of understanding promotion.[11] Nevertheless, the idea that the relevant kind of promotion is probabilistic is controversial. Though many writers are tempted by this sort of probability-raising view, others doubt that reasons can be helpfully analyzed in terms of probabilities.[12] Fortunately, my project here does not depend on any particular view about what it is to promote an objective. Before moving on to argue against various non-contrastive theories, I will just list some structural properties that I will assume the relevant kind of promotion has. It will be clear that a probability-raising analysis of promotion will have these properties, but I will not assume such an analysis.

The basic idea is that reasons are tied to promotion of objectives. On many versions of this idea, what matters is *whether* the action in question promotes an objective. As we will see shortly, it is not straightforward to say what it takes for an action to promote an objective categorically. My view will instead be framed in terms of *how well* an action promotes an objective. This may seem to require first saying what it is for an action to promote an objective at all. But another way of understanding my view is as saying that whether an action promotes an objective at all, in the sense relevant for a theory of reasons, will depend on comparative facts. For example, on a probabilistic view, whether an action promotes an objective will depend on comparisons of how much the relevant actions raise the probability of the objective. Nevertheless, it will

---

[10] See Finlay (2006, 2014), Schroeder (2007), Bedke (2012), Kolodny (forthcoming) for different versions of this idea.

[11] Since I began writing this book, a small cottage industry has grown up around this question, arguably beginning with Behrends and DiPaolo (2011). See also Coates (2014), Sharadin (2015), Lin (2016), for a sampling.

[12] See Wedgwood (2009), Sharadin (2015), for example.

be easier to present the view as if we already have an understanding of what it takes for an action to promote an objective in the first place, and focus instead on comparisons of how well the actions promote the objectives.

With these qualifications in mind, the first assumption I will make is that the relevant kind of promotion *ranks* actions in terms of how well they promote the objective. Different objectives will of course give us different rankings: A-ing may promote objective O better than B-ing, while B-ing promotes objective Y better than A-ing. These rankings may allow for both ties and incommensurability. But I do assume that the ranking is transitive: if A better promotes O than B, and B better promotes O than C, then A better promotes O than C. (In formal terms, I will assume that a given objective *partially orders* actions in terms of how well they promote the objective.) I will not argue for this property here. But I do think that this is a pretty minimal assumption. Moreover, the popular probability-raising view of promotion will have this property. We can rank actions in terms of how much they raise the probability of the objective. And, if A raises the probability of O more than B, and B raises the probability of O more than C, then A will raise the probability of O more than C, since 'greater than' is transitive.

The second assumption I will make is that this ranking will have what I call the **Disjunction Boundedness** property:

**Disjunction Boundedness:** For all actions A and B and for all objectives O, $A \vee B$ is ranked somewhere between (inclusive) A and B, in terms of how well it promotes O.

This property is less familiar than the ranking property I introduced in the previous paragraph. But, again, I think it is very plausible that any reasonable understanding of the relevant kind of promotion will have this property. Doing $A \vee B$ cannot do more than both A and B to help bring about an objective, and similarly it cannot do less than both. The probability-raising understanding of promotion has this property.[13]

---

[13] It is a fact about conditional probabilities that when $P(X|A) \geq P(X|B)$, $P(X|A) \geq P(X|A \vee B) \geq P(X|B)$. So doing $A \vee B$ cannot make O more probable than doing A or less probable than doing B.

Now I will discuss some non-contrastive views about the relationship between promotion and reasons. I will argue that all of them are problematic, which motivates my contrastive theory.[14]

### 4.2.2 Doing nothing

The first view I'll consider is offered by Schroeder (2007: 113):

> **Doing Nothing:** $s$ has a reason to $A$ provided by objective $O$ iff $s$'s $A$-ing would promote $O$ better than $s$'s doing nothing would.

One important question for this view is what it is to *do nothing*. But the central problem, raised by Evers (2009), is that, no matter how we understand doing nothing, it seems that there will be possible cases in which agents have reasons to do nothing. For example, doing nothing may just be maintaining the status quo (this is at least suggested by Schroeder). But sometimes we have reasons simply to maintain the status quo; similar remarks go for other natural ways of understanding what it is to do nothing. But it is easy to see that this view rules this out: for me to have a reason to do nothing, according to this view, my doing nothing would have to promote some objective better than my doing nothing would. And of course this is impossible.

### 4.2.3 Not A-ing

The second view I will consider is offered by Finlay (2006, 2014):

> **Not A:** $s$ has a reason to $A$ provided by $O$ iff $s$'s $A$-ing better promotes $O$ than $s$'s not $A$-ing.

This account allows for reasons to do nothing: you can have such a reason as long as your doing nothing promotes some objective better than *not* doing nothing. But to evaluate this account, we need to know what not $A$-ing is. Here are three options:

> **Possibilism:** $s$ has a reason to $A$ provided by $O$ iff $s$'s $A$-ing better promotes $O$ than everything else $s$ could do.

---

[14] The non-contrastive views I will consider were originally offered in probabilistic terms, but I will abstract away from this and just discuss them in terms of a more abstract notion of promotion. This is fine for my purposes, since I am interested in what these views say about the relationship between promotion and reasons, not in the particular way they understand promotion.

**Actualism:** $s$ has a reason to $A$ provided by $O$ iff $s$'s $A$-ing better promotes $O$ than whatever it is $s$ would actually do, if she did not $A$.

**Probabilism:** $s$ has a reason to $A$ provided by $O$ iff $s$'s $A$-ing better promotes $O$ than $s$'s not $A$-ing, where the degree to which $s$'s not $A$-ing promotes $O$ is a function of (i) the degree to which $s$'s $B$-ing promotes $O$, and (ii) the probability that $s$ will perform $B$, for each alternative $B$ incompatible with $A$.

**Possibilism** says that, for $O$ to give you a reason to $A$, your $A$-ing has to better promote $O$ than everything else you could do. **Actualism** says that your $A$-ing just has to promote $O$ better than whatever it is you'd actually do, if you didn't do $A$.[15] **Probabilism** appeals to a kind of expected value, as far as $O$ goes, of not $A$-ing by weighting the degree to which each other option $B$ promotes $O$ by the probability that you'll actually perform that option $B$.[16]

Each of these proposals is quite natural. But all of them suffer from the same basic problem. Consider the following simple case, offered by Behrends and DiPaolo (2011). Debbie has a choice between pushing one of three buttons, A, B, and C. If Debbie pushes either A or B, her desire for $p$ will be satisfied. If she pushes C, it will not. Suppose that Debbie actually pushes A, and that, if she had not pushed A, she would have pushed B.

According to **Possibilism**, Debbie's desire that $p$ gave her no reason to push button A, since it did not better promote the object of that desire than something else she could have done, namely pushing button B—either way, her desire that $p$ would have been satisfied.

Similarly, according to **Actualism**, her desire that $p$ gave her no reason to push button A, since doing so did not better promote the object of the desire than doing what she would have done, had she not pushed button A—namely, pushing button B.

Things are a bit more complicated with **Probabilism**. But we can describe the case (or at least a similar case) and stipulate some values for

---

[15] The labels 'Possibilism' and 'Actualism' are familiar from the literature on moral obligation; see Jackson and Pargetter (1986).

[16] This view is much more amenable to a probabilistic view of promotion; at the very least, the weighting is straightforward, since we can just calculate the relevant probabilities. Without assuming this probabilistic view, though, it would take some work to spell out just how the weighting will work. Rather than veering way from the main discussion in this way, though, I will trust that the idea is clear enough.

the probabilities that Debbie takes each of the options.[17] If we are careful in setting things up, we will be able to describe a case in which, according to **Probabilism**, Debbie's desire that $p$ again gives her no reason to push button A.[18]

So all three versions of **Not A**—**Possibilism**, **Actualism**, and **Probabilism**—are committed to saying that Debbie's desire that $p$ gave her no reason to push button A whatsoever. But clearly this desire gave her a reason to push button A *rather than* push button C. On a non-contrastive view like **Not A**, though, it is hard to see how Debbie's desire that $p$ could give her a reason to push A rather than push C if it gives her *no reason whatsoever* to push A. So **Not A** appears to make it too hard to have reasons to do things—there are cases in which agents clearly have reasons to do $A$ rather than $B$, but this theory—on at least three very natural precisifications—says that the agent has no reason whatsoever to do $A$.[19]

### 4.2.4 Contrastive promotion

The lesson to draw from the problems facing the different versions of **Not A**, I suggest, is that the relevant sort of promotion is contrastive. Even if doing $A$ does not better promote some objective than *everything* else you could do, or even better than what you would actually do if you did

---

[17] Finlay (2014) gives a kind of Probabilist view of 'ought', but makes an assumption that he labels the 'Symmetry of Choice', whereby we assume that the agent is equally likely to take each option available to her. Finlay's view will suffer from the same problem as **Probabilism**.

[18] If we assume the probabilistic understanding of promotion, here is a counterexample. Suppose the relevant objective is my getting Thai food ($T$), and there are three options: go to Thai Patio, go to RCA, go to Zankou Chicken. Suppose that there is a 60% chance I go to Thai Patio, a 30% chance I go to RCA, and a 10% chance I go to Zankou Chicken. And suppose $P(T|$ I go to Thai Patio$)= 0.9$, $P(T|$ I go to RCA$)= 0.2$, and $P(T|$ I go to Zankou Chicken$)= 0$. We end up with the result that $P(T|$ I do not go to RCA$)$ is roughly 0.77, which is greater than $P(T|$ I go to RCA$)= 0.2$. Thus, according to this view, my desire for Thai food gives me no reason at all to go to RCA, even though I clearly have a reason to go to RCA rather than go to Zankou Chicken. Both **Actualism** and **Possibilism** will also have problems with this case (assuming I will actually go to Thai Patio if I don't go to RCA). This shows that the argument against those views does not depend on there being ties, as in Behrends and DiPaolo's button-pushing case.

[19] The reader may be wondering about a version of **Possibilism** on which we replace 'everything' with 'something'—that is, $O$ gives you a reason to $A$ when your $A$-ing better promotes $O$ than *something* else you can do. This view would avoid the problem facing the three versions of **Not A** I have considered so far. The argument against this view is slightly more complicated, but the problem will become clear later, when I introduce my own contrastive analysis of reasons for; see n. 29. To anticipate: the basic problem is that we get a violation of the principle I called **Restricted Exclusivity** in Chapter 2.

not *A*, for example, it can still better promote it than some other option, *B*. What we have seen is that, in these cases, the objective clearly gives you reasons to do *A* rather than *B*. The challenge for the non-contrastivist is to explain how this could be true even though, according to those views, you have no reason to do *A* whatsoever. The contrastivist, on the other hand, can simply say that you have reasons to do *A* rather than *B*, even if you don't have reasons to do *A* rather than some *other* option *C*. By relativizing reasons to sets that are not necessarily exhaustive of every possibility open to the agent, then, the contrastivist avoids the problems facing non-contrastive theories. In Section 4.3, I will develop this thought into a detailed version of contrastivism.

### 4.2.5 Motivating resolution sensitivity

The arguments against the non-contrastive accounts of reasons in terms of promotion illustrate the advantages of non-exhaustivity. But when I introduced contrastivism in Chapter 1, I pointed out a second feature of the view—namely, resolution sensitivity. This is the idea that reasons can vary between sets that differ in how the possibilities are lumped together, for example, between {go to work, stay home} and {drive to work, take the bus to work, stay home and cook, stay home and nap}. The arguments I've given so far don't motivate this feature of contrastivism. But once we relativize reasons to sets of alternatives, there are cases in which whether or not something is a reason for an action seems to depend not just on what possibilities are covered by the alternatives in the set, but also on how we group those possibilities into alternatives.

Consider the following version of the famous Professor Procrastinate case from Jackson (1985) and Jackson and Pargetter (1986). Professor Procrastinate has been asked to write a review of an important new book, because she is the most qualified person to write it. But she is a terrible procrastinator. If she accepts the invitation, she is very unlikely to write the review. And, if that happens, the author's career and the field at large will suffer. If Procrastinate just declines the invitation, someone else—less qualified, but more reliable—will be asked to write, and will do so. In this case, the fact that Procrastinate is a procrastinator is a reason for her to decline the invitation rather than accept. That is, it's a reason to decline out of {decline, accept}, plausibly provided by the objective of doing what's best for the profession. But it is intuitively not a reason to decline out of the more fine-grained set, {decline, accept and write, accept and don't write}.[20] So whether or not this fact is a reason to decline seems to depend on the resolution at which we divide up the alternatives. Thus, once we relativize reasons to sets of alternatives, there's good reason to allow the sets to vary in resolution, rather than, say, making them all maximally fine-grained.

## 4.3 Contrastive Reasons and Promotion

I have argued that the relationship between reasons and promotion is best understood contrastively. An objective can give you reasons to perform an action $A$ relative to a set of alternatives when your $A$-ing promotes that objective better than anything else in the set. In this section, I will begin to develop this idea into a more detailed contrastive account of reasons.

**Promote** tells us what has to hold for you to have a reason to $A$, or for there to be a reason for you to $A$. But we want an account of when some fact is a reason for you to $A$. Philosophers who appeal to promotion to analyze the reason relation frequently appeal to *explanation* here. If you have a reason to $A$ because $A$-ing promotes some objective, then some fact is a reason for you to $A$ when it *explains why* (or is an essential part of the explanation for why) $A$-ing promotes the objective. Like most of these other writers, I take the relevant sort of explanation here to be a non-epistemic notion. For $r$ to explain why your $A$-ing would promote $O$ is for $r$ to be part of what makes it true that your $A$-ing would promote $O$.[21] I have a reason to go to the store because doing so would promote the objective of my having breakfast in the morning. The fact that I'm out of milk is part of the explanation for why going to the store would promote this objective. So, according to this idea, the fact that I'm out of milk is a reason to go to the store.

So what we want is a contrastivist analysis of reasons for and reasons against in terms of promotion. So far I have said that $r$ is a reason for you to $A$ out of $Q$ when it helps explain why your $A$-ing would promote some objective better than other alternatives in $Q$. Conversely, it is natural to think that $r$ is a reason *against* $A$-ing out of $Q$ when it helps explain

---

[20] Remember that the option is 'accept and write', not 'try to accept and write' or 'agree to accept and write'. And, by hypothesis, accepting and writing is better than declining, even if accepting is not better than declining. This is what is interesting and somewhat puzzling about this case, and why it motivates resolution sensitivity.

[21] For analyses of reasons partly in terms of explanation, see Toulmin (1950), Finlay (2001, 2006, 2014), Searle (2001), Broome (2004), Schroeder (2007).

why *A*-ing would promote some objective *less well* than other alternatives in *Q*.

First a quick note about reasons against. It is often thought that a reason against some action *A* is just a reason for not-*A*.[22] On this view, we can just have one kind of reason, reasons for. But the contrastivist cannot accept this view because, given non-exhaustivity, the sets of alternatives to which reasons are relativized need not be closed under negation: just because *A* is in a set, it does not follow that not-*A* is also in the set. So, if we want to talk about reasons against an alternative *A* relative to a set *Q*, we can't just talk about the reasons for not-*A* out of *Q*, since not-*A* might not even be in *Q*. Thus, the contrastivist needs to define reasons against—reasons not to *A*, instead of reasons to not-*A*—separately.

So start (for expositional purposes) with reasons against. I suggest the following analysis:

**Against:** *r* is a reason against *A*-ing out of *Q* iff there's some *O* of the relevant kind[23] such that *r* explains why[24] *B*-ing better promotes *O* than *A*-ing, for some other alternative *B* in *Q*.[25]

If you could do better, as far as *O* is concerned, by doing something other than *A*-ing, then *O* very plausibly gives you a reason against *A*-ing. An obvious alternative to **Against** would say that your *A*-ing has to do worse at promoting *O* than *all* the other alternatives. But this misses out on some intuitive reasons against. For example, suppose I can travel the fifteen miles to campus by jogging, biking, or driving. The fact that I want to get there in under an hour intuitively gives me a reason against biking, even though I have a better chance of getting there in under an

---

[22] See, e.g., Nagel (1970: 47 n. 1), and Schroeder (2007: ch. 7).

[23] Recall that by 'some *O* of the relevant kind', I mean the following: there's some set of objectives that are the things to be promoted, according to our theory of reasons. A desire-based theory will say that this set contains objects of the desires of the agent; a value-based theory will say that it contains some independent values. *O* is an objective of the relevant kind when it is in this set. By existentially quantifying here, we allow that there are multiple objectives that can give you reasons in any individual case.

[24] Or is part of the explanation of why—I'll ignore this qualification from now on.

[25] Here is the version we would get if we assumed the popular probability-raising view of promotion letting *O* stand for a proposition that's suitably related to the objective (e.g., the proposition desired, the proposition that the value is realized).

**Against Prob:** *r* is a reason against *A*-ing out of *Q* iff there's some *O* of the relevant kind such that *r* explains why $P(O|\text{you } A) < P(O|\text{you } B)$, for some other alternative *B* in *Q*.

hour if I bike than if I jog—it's still quite unlikely that I get there in under an hour if I bike.

Once we accept **Against** as an analysis of reasons against, I think we should accept the following analysis of reasons for:

> **For:** $r$ is a reason for you to $A$ out of $Q$ iff there's some $O$ of the relevant kind such that $r$ explains why $A$-ing better promotes $O$ than $B$, for all the other alternatives $B$ in $Q$.[26]

This makes reasons for harder to come by than reasons against. But I think this is a very plausible analysis of reasons for. If you could do better, as far as $O$ is concerned, by doing something other than $A$-ing, it would be strange if $O$ gave you a reason to $A$ out of a set of alternatives that includes that other thing.[27]

The most natural alternative would say that $O$ can give you a reason to $A$ relative to some set when your $A$-ing would better promote $O$ than *some* other alternative in the set. This would capture the reasonable idea that a consideration can be a reason for multiple members of the same set, but a *weightier* reason only for those that better promote the relevant objective.[28] But, if we accept this in addition to **Against**, we get a violation of the principle from Chapter 2 that I called **Restricted Exclusivity**. Some consideration $r$ could be both a reason for and a reason against all the alternatives in the middle—that do not do the best and that do not do the worst, in terms of promoting $O$. For example, in the case I introduced above, the fact that campus is fifteen miles away would be both a reason to bike and a reason not to bike, both provided by my desire to get to campus in under an hour. As I argued in Chapter 2, violations of this principle are implausible.[29]

---

[26] Probabilistic version:
> **For Prob:** $r$ is a reason for you to $A$ out of $Q$ iff there's some $O$ of the relevant kind and $r$ explains why $P(O|\text{you } A) > P(O|\text{you } B)$, for all $B \neq A$ in $Q$.

[27] Interestingly, though I reject Finlay's non-contrastive account of reasons (2014), this contrastive account of reasons for closely mirrors his contrastive analysis of 'ought'. According to that analysis, roughly, you ought to $A$ just in case your $A$-ing makes the contextually salient end more likely than any other relevant alternative. By allowing multiple objectives—the analog of Finlay's ends—to provide reasons in a single context, my analysis is better suited to the *pro tanto* notion of a reason.

[28] I want to emphasize here that **For** and **Against** are accounts of when some consideration is a reason for an action; for all I have said, they have nothing at all to say about the *weight* of those reasons, or what you have *most* reason to do.

[29] This argument also tells against a revised version of **Possibilism**, mentioned in n. 19, according to which an objective provides a reason for you to $A$ when $A$-ing better promotes an objective than *something*—instead of *everything*—else you could do.

A concern about this picture involves cases in which two alternatives from a set do an equally good job promoting a given objective. Suppose that some objective $O$ would be equally well promoted either by $A$-ing or by $B$-ing. According to **For**, $O$ does not give me any reason to $A$ or any reason to $B$, relative to a set that includes both, like $\{A, B, C\}$. This is a bit counterintuitive; it seems that $O$ could give us reasons for both $A$ and $B$, rather than neither. This suggests replacing **For** with a principle that says that $r$ is a reason for $A$ out of $Q$ when $A$ promotes some objective *at least as well as* any other member of $Q$. The primary reason I do not adopt this principle is that it does not allow us to capture all of the entailment relations between reasons relative to different sets that I think we need to capture; we'll be able to see this more clearly later, once I show how the account I favor—combining **Against** and **For**—can capture them.

Moreover, I think we can mitigate the counterintuitiveness of the claim that, when $A$ and $B$ equally well promote some objective, that objective doesn't provide reasons for either of them relative to a set that includes both. First, it is not at all counterintuitive to deny that the objective provides reasons for $A$ rather than $B$ (or for $B$ rather than $A$)—that is, for $A$ (or $B$) relative to $\{A, B\}$. And this is because $A$ and $B$ do an equally good job promoting the objective. Thus, it would be strange to put this consideration forward as supporting one of them. So perhaps it is not so bad to say that it does not provide reasons for $A$ out of $\{A, B, C\}$. After all, you could just as easily promote the objective by doing $B$ instead, and $B$ is a relevant alternative.[30] Second, the objective does provide reasons both for $A$ rather than $C$ and for $B$ rather than $C$. Third, given **Against**, the objective gives you reasons *against* $C$ out of $\{A, B, C\}$, but does not give you reasons against either $A$ or $B$. And finally, as we will see later, on my view, we can say that the objective gives you reasons for $A \vee B$ out of the closely related set, $\{A \vee B, C\}$. Given these considerations, and the fact that the suggested replacement for **For** misses out on some intuitive entailment relations that **For** can capture, I will stick with the **For** formulation.

---

[30] We may add that $A$ must also do better than some member of $Q$, to avoid saying that $r$ is a reason to $A$ rather than $B$ (or to $A$ out of $\{A, B\}$) when $A$ and $B$ promote the relevant objective equally well. But the point is just that, since the objective does not provide reasons relative to $\{A, B\}$, perhaps it isn't so bad to deny that it provides reasons relative to larger sets that include both $A$ and $B$.

Another potential objection to this view is that its treatment of reasons against is too liberal. A reason against some alternative, you might think, has to "imply a significant criticism" of that alternative, to borrow a phrase from Greenspan (2005, 2007), and merely being a reason for an incompatible alternative isn't enough. But other philosophers seem to agree with me that a reason for one alternative is in fact a reason against incompatible alternatives, for some relatively weak notion of incompatibility, such as physical or psychological incompatibility.[31] If some consideration $r$ is a reason for $A$—if it highlights some benefit of doing $A$—and if doing $B$ precludes doing $A$, then it is very plausible that $r$ is a reason against $B$, since doing $B$ would keep you from getting that benefit. This is just the familiar notion of an *opportunity cost*: among the costs of—or reasons against—choices you make are the benefits you sacrifice that would come from making other choices.

Note, though, that we can draw an interesting distinction between two types of reasons against on this view. A reason against some alternative that does imply a significant criticism of that alternative—like the fact that Zankou Chicken is really crowded at this time of day—often won't turn out to be a reason for any other particular alternative. That's because these sorts of facts are often irrelevant for differences between other alternatives in the set. For example, the fact that Zankou Chicken is really crowded doesn't tell us anything about the relationship between going to Thai Patio and going to Spicy Thai BBQ. So it doesn't explain why going to Thai Patio better promotes my desire not to wait than going to Spicy Thai BBQ, or vice versa. So by **For**, it won't turn out to be a reason for either of these, though it's still a reason against going to Zankou Chicken. Reasons against an alternative that do not imply a significant criticism, on the other hand, will often be reasons for other particular alternatives. So, even on this view, we can capture Greenspan's insight: some considerations merely count against certain alternatives without counting in favor of others.

---

[31] Sinnott-Armstrong (2008: 258) says that a reason "favors one thing and disfavors others." Ruben (2009: 63) says that when doing $A$ is incompatible with doing $B$, "a reason to do an act of type $B$ must also be a reason not to do an action of type $A$". And Broome (2013: 56) cites nice features of one alternative—which are reasons for taking that alternative—as reasons against incompatible alternatives. Compare the discussion of 'General Substitutability' in Sinnott-Armstrong (1992: sect. 1).

## 4.4 Contrastive Reasons as Better Reasons?

In Chapter 2, I argued that we cannot understand explicitly contrastive reason ascriptions like '*r* is a reason to *A* rather than *B*' in terms of the strength of reasons, as in '*r* is a stronger reason to *A* than to *B*'. First, this relies on an ad hoc treatment of the phrase 'rather than' in reason ascriptions. In other uses, 'rather than' means something along the lines of 'and not', and is used to introduce alternatives. In no other uses does it mean 'stronger than'. Moreover, there are cases in which a claim like '*r* is a reason to *A* rather than *B*' is true, where the truth of this claim is explained by some objective (for example, my desire not to wear myself out getting to campus), while '*r* is a reason not to *A*' is also true, and is also explained by the same objective. As long as '*r* is a reason to *A* rather than *B*' entails '*r* is a reason to *A*', as it must, on this view—if r is a stronger reason to *A* than to *B*, then it must be a reason to *A*, according to the non-contrastivist— we have an implausible violation of the principle **Restricted Exclusivity**. This principle says that it's impossible for one fact to be both a reason to *A* and a reason not to *A*, where both are explained by the same objective.

I gave similar arguments against a related, but more subtle, view in Chapter 3. This view (stated in Chapter 3 in terms of favoring, now stated in terms of reasons) introduced the terminology of *O*-favoring, from which we naturally get an idea of an *O*-reason—a reason explained by objective *O*. According to this view, *r* is a reason to *A* rather than *B*, explained by objective *O*, when there is no fact that is a better *O*-reason to *B* than *r* is to *A*.

The contrastive theory I have developed in this chapter has certain affinities with these views. This is not surprising, since, as a contrastive theory, it holds that reasons are to be understood partly in terms of comparisons of contrasting alternatives. This theory says that *r* is a reason to *A*, relative to a set of alternatives *Q*, explained or provided by objective *O*, when *r* explains why *A*-ing better promotes *O* than any other alternative in *Q*. The important difference between this theory and the earlier, non-contrastive theories is that the comparison shows up in the analysis of what it is for some consideration to be a reason, and is a comparison of how well the contrasting actions promote the relevant objective.

The non-contrastive theories, on the other hand, appeal to comparisons between the strengths of the reasons themselves. Thus, they are committed to reading the 'rather than' in contrastive reason ascriptions as 'stronger than', while the contrastive theory need not do this. 'Rather than' can be treated as it normally is, as introducing alternatives.

The contrastive theory also avoids commitment to the inference from '*r* is a reason to *A* rather than *B*' to '*r* is a reason to *A*', as I explained in Chapter 2. Thus, we will not get violations of **Restricted Exclusivity**, relative to a given set of alternatives. In fact, the contrastive theory explains why **Restricted Exclusivity** is a true principle about reasons: when *r* is a reason for an action out of a set of alternatives, explained by *O*, that means that the action better promotes *O* than any other alternative in the set. For *r* also to be a reason against the action relative to that set, explained by *O*, the action would have to promote *O* less well than some other alternative. But this is impossible, given that it promotes *O* better than any other alternative. We can, of course, get violations of the false principle, **Exclusivity**, which says that, if a fact is a reason to *A*, it is not also a reason not to *A*. Contrastivism does not support this principle, since *A*-ing may promote one objective better than any other alternative in the set, but promote another objective less well than some other alternative, where both of these promotion facts are explained by the same fact.

## 4.5 Providing the Constraints

In this section, I'll show that this contrastive theory, independently motivated by considerations about the relationship between reasons and promotion, straightforwardly provides the constraints on the independence of reasons relative to different sets of alternatives I motivated in Section 4.1, as well as some other interesting and intuitive constraints.

### 4.5.1 Transitivity

The first constraint we need on the independence of reasons relative to different sets is one that rules out the sort of intransitivity I described in Section 4.1.1. That is, we want it to turn out that, whenever *r* is a reason for *A* rather than *B* and for *B* rather than *C*, it is also a reason for *A* rather than *C*. In fact, we need an importantly but subtly different constraint, once we adopt a view on which we explain reasons in terms of the promotion of various kinds of objectives. We don't just want reasons for *A* rather than *B* and for *B* rather than *C* to be reasons for *A* rather than *C*; we want them to be provided by the same objective. A case in which my desire for Thai food gives me a reason $r$ for $A$ rather than $B$ and for $B$ rather than $C$, but not for $A$ rather than $C$, is counter to the transitivity intuition, even if, say, my desire to spend lots of money explains why $r$ is a reason for $A$ rather than $C$.

So what we need is the following kind of constraint:

**Transitivity:** If $r$ is a reason for $A$ rather than $B$, explained by objective $O$, and a reason for $B$ rather than $C$, explained by $O$, then $r$ is a reason for $A$ rather than $C$, explained by $O$.

Fortunately, it is easy to see that this follows straightforwardly from the framework I developed in the previous section. Recall the minimal assumptions I am making about the promotion relation relevant for **Promote**—for an analysis of reasons. In particular, I am assuming that the promotion relation ranks alternatives in terms of how well they promote a given objective (so each objective gives us a different promotion ranking); this ranking, I assumed, is transitive.[32] Thus, if $A$ better promotes $O$ than $B$, and $B$ better promotes $O$ than $C$, then $A$ better promotes $O$ than $C$. And, given plausible assumptions about how explanation works in these cases—namely, that, if $r$ explains both why $A$ better promotes $O$ than $B$ and why $B$ better promotes $O$ than $C$, then it also explains why $A$ better promotes $O$ than $C$—$r$ explains this.[33] Finally, given **For**, **Transitivity** follows.

### 4.5.2 Non-exhaustivity

Now I'll discuss other entailments between reasons relative to sets that differ in the alternatives they include—that is, sets that differ along the dimension of non-exhaustivity.

First, consider reasons for an alternative relative to one set, and reasons for that alternative relative to a subset of that initial set. I said in section 4.1.2 that, intuitively, facts that are reasons for $A$ relative to $Q$ should also be reasons for $A$ relative to subsets of $Q$ that contain $A$. Suppose that this were not true. Then there might be a case in which $r$ is a reason for $A$

---

[32] As I have pointed out, the popular probability-raising view of promotion gives us this property, simply because the greater than relation is transitive. We can see this clearly by looking at the probabilistic version of **For** given in n. 26.

[33] Remember that I'm using a non-epistemic notion of explanation here. Perhaps the epistemic notion will not have this feature, but the sense I intend, on which $x$ explains $y$ when $x$ is part of what makes it true that $y$, plausibly does.

rather than either of B or C, but not a reason for A rather than B. It's implausible that there could be such a case, so we should rule it out.

Fortunately, the theory I developed in the previous Section 4.3—in particular **For**—delivers precisely this result. If r is a reason for A out of Q, explained by objective O, then, by **For**, r explains why A promotes O better than B, for all the other alternatives B in Q. Since the degree to which actions promote objectives does not vary with the alternatives, A will promote O better than B for all the alternatives B in any subset of Q. Given the same kinds of assumptions as those we have made about explanation, r will explain this. So r will be a reason for A out of any subset of Q that contains A.

Next, consider reasons against. I have said that reasons against an alternative out of one set should also be reasons against that alternative out of supersets of the initial set. If this entailment did not hold, then we might have a case like the following. r is a reason against A when the alternative is B alone, but not a reason against A when we consider C in addition to B. Again, this is implausible. Introducing a new alternative may introduce new reasons against existing options, but it should not eliminate existing reasons against.

Fortunately, the theory delivers just the result we want. Suppose r is a reason against A out of Q, explained by O. Then, by **Against**, some other alternative in Q better promotes O than A. Merely adding some new alternatives to Q won't change this fact: the alternatives that better promote O than A will still do so. Thus, r will also be a reason against A relative to the new superset of Q. So the independently motivated version of contrastivism that analyzes reasons in terms of promotion delivers precisely the constraints we need, on the independence of reasons relative to sets and their subsets and supersets.[34]

### 4.5.3 Resolution sensitivity

I also introduced a second feature of contrastivism, which I labeled resolution sensitivity. Two sets of alternatives may cover the same possibilities, but do so at different levels of detail. For example, we might have reasons to A relative to a more fine-grained set like $\{A, B, C\}$ or relative to the more coarse-grained set $\{A, B \vee C\}$. The second set divides up the

---

[34] Compare the discussion of choice functions in Sen (1971). The constraints I have discussed here mirror constraints on rational choice functions that Sen proposes.

possibilities in a more coarse-grained way, by grouping together the *B* and *C* possibilities. Now I will suggest that there should be constraints on how reasons can vary as the resolution differs, and show that the theory I have developed delivers them.

Suppose the fact that I don't have any vacation days left is a reason to go to work out of {go to work, stay home and clean, stay home and watch TV, stay home and do something else}, explained by my desire not to get fired. Then it is also a reason to go to work out of the more coarse-grained set {go to work, stay home}. If doing *A* is better, with respect to the objective *O*, than all of the (relevant) ways of doing *B*, then doing *A* is obviously better than doing *B*, as far as *O* is concerned. So reasons for an alternative out of one set should also be reasons for that alternative out of sets that group together the other alternatives, resulting in a more coarse-grained set.

Next, consider reasons against. The fact that I am out of vacation days is a reason against staying home out of the relatively coarse-grained set {go to work, stay home}. It is also a reason against staying home out of the more fine-grained set {go to work by car, go to work by bus, go to work some other way, stay home}. So reasons against an alternative out of one set should also be reasons against that alternative out of sets that separate the other alternatives into more fine-grained alternatives.

Recall that, in addition to the assumption that the promotion relation provides us with a ranking of alternatives, I also assumed that the ranking has a special property called **Disjunction Boundedness**:

> **Disjunction Boundedness:** For all actions *A* and *B* and for all objectives *O*, $A \vee B$ is ranked somewhere between (inclusive) *A* and *B*, in terms of how well it promotes *O*.

The intuitive thought here is simply that doing $A \vee B$ cannot do better than both *A* and *B*, or worse than both *A* and *B*, at promoting a given objective—doing $A \vee B$ requires doing one or the other, after all. So I think this is a very safe assumption.[35]

Fortunately, this safe assumption is just what we need to secure the entailment relations between reasons relative to sets that differ in resolution. When *r* is a reason for *A* out of {*A*, *B*, *C*}, provided by *O*, that

---

[35] As I have pointed out, the popular probability-raising view of promotion gives us this property, because it is a fact about conditional probability that, where $P(X|A) > P(X|B)$, $P(X|A) \geq P(X|A \vee B) \geq P(X|B)$.

means it promotes $O$ better than either $B$ or $C$, by **For**. Given **Disjunction Boundedness** and **For**, then, $r$ will also be a reason for $A$ out of the more coarse-grained set $\{A, B \vee C\}$.

Suppose that $r$ is a reason against $A$ out of $\{A, B\}$. That means it does a worse job promoting $O$ than $B$. Now suppose we divide $B$ into more fine-grained alternatives, say $C$ and $D$, to obtain the more fine-grained set $\{A, C, D\}$, where $B = C \vee D$. We know by **Disjunction Boundedness** that $B$ cannot be ranked above both of $C$ and $D$. Since $A$ is ranked below $B$, then $A$ must be ranked below at least one of $C$ and $D$. So, by **Against**, $r$ will be a reason against $A$ out of $\{A, C, D\}$.[36]

I've shown that the contrastive theory of reasons I developed in the previous section straightforwardly provides just the right constraints on the independence of reasons relative to different sets. I'll now show that the theory also provides other interesting constraints that are less obvious, but no less intuitive, once they're in view, than the ones I've discussed.

### 4.5.4 Other entailments: Unions and intersections

The last set of constraints delivered by the theory that I will discuss involve unions and intersections of sets of alternatives. As I said, these constraints are less obvious than those I have discussed so far. But I think they are very plausible. This provides additional confirmation for the theory, since it not only delivers the obvious constraints, but brings other plausible constraints into view.

First, note that the following two constraints follow as corollaries of the previous ones involving subsets and supersets. (i) Reasons for $A$ out of both $Q$ and $Q'$, both provided by $O$, will be reasons for $A$ out of the intersection, $Q \cap Q'$, provided by $O$. This just follows from the result that reasons for $A$ out of one set are reasons for $A$ out of subsets of that set.[37]

---

[36] We might also wonder about the relationship between reasons for $A$ relative to one set and reasons for more coarse-grained alternatives that subsume $A$ (say, $A \vee B$) in more coarse-grained sets of alternatives. Similarly, we might wonder about the relationship between reasons for a more coarse-grained alternative (say, $A \vee B$) and reasons for the fine-grained alternatives that it subsumes (say, $A$) relative to more fine-grained sets. It turns out that the theory doesn't deliver any constraints in these cases. I think these are the intuitively correct results, though I won't argue for that here.

[37] The limiting case here is when $Q \cap Q' = \{A\}$. Technically, by **For**, everything will be a reason for $A$ relative to this singleton set. But singleton sets will never be the relevant set—if there's only one relevant alternative, then there's no need for deliberation, and there won't be reasons for or against the single alternative.

(ii) Reasons against $A$ out of both $Q$ and $Q'$ will be reasons against $A$ out of the union, $Q \cup Q'$. This just follows from the result that reasons against $A$ out of one set are reasons against $A$ out of supersets, as well.

We also get the following new result, which is not simply a corollary of a previous one. Suppose $r$ is a reason to $A$ out of $Q$, provided by $O$, and that $r$ is also a reason to $A$ out of $Q'$, provided by $O$. What about the *union* of these two sets, $Q \cup Q'$? By **For**, we can immediately see that $r$ will be a reason for $A$ relative to the union, as well. And this seems correct: if nothing in either set was better than $A$, as far as $O$ is concerned, then putting them all together in the same set should not make a difference.[38] Interestingly, we don't get the corresponding result for reasons against and intersections: it's not true in general that, if $r$ is a reason against $A$ out of $Q$ and out of $Q'$, then it's a reason against $A$ out of $Q \cap Q'$, since we may lose all of the alternatives in either set that are ranked higher than $A$, when we intersect the two sets.

## 4.6 Non-Promotional Reasons

So far, I have argued that the widespread idea that reasons involve promotion supports a particular version of contrastivism that delivers intuitive constraints on how reasons can vary with the alternatives. In doing so, I have assumed that all reasons involve promotion of the sort I have been discussing. In this section I will show how to relax that assumption.

In Section 4.2, I argued that, even if we think that some reasons do not involve promotion, but rather involve respecting or honoring values, my argument that the reasons that do involve promotion are contrastive puts rational pressure on us to adopt contrastivism about all reasons. But there is still a serious gap. I've spent the last few sections showing how a contrastive theory of reasons cashed out in terms of promotion straightforwardly delivers important constraints on how reasons can vary with sets of alternatives. In doing so, I made crucial use of rankings of alternatives in terms of how well they promote various objectives. But, if

---

[38] One complication is that the alternatives in $Q$ may not all be incompatible with or identical to the alternatives in $Q'$—the alternatives may partially overlap, in a sense. In that case, we will not be able to look at $Q \cup Q'$, since that won't qualify as a set of alternatives. Instead, we'll have to look at a related set that results from regrouping the possibilities to eliminate this partial overlap.

some reasons do not involve the promotion of objectives at all, how can we provide the constraints for these reasons? Moreover, if we need to tell some other story for these reasons, there's a worry that it will generalize to explain the constraints on how the reasons that do involve promotion can vary. This would undermine my claim that the idea that reasons involve promotion and contrastivism about reasons are mutually supporting.

Fortunately, I think we can generalize the explanation of the constraints given in terms of promotion. The basic idea is that different alternatives can do better or worse at respecting or honoring values. For example, going into the burning building to save someone better respects the value of human life than merely calling the fire department, which in turn is better than just walking by without even calling. There may be various ways of being better at respecting or honoring some value. For example, one action may respect a given value *more* than another action, or one action may be *closer to the ideal* way of honoring a given value than another action. The important point is that we will still be able to get a ranking of alternatives, not in terms of how well they promote a given value, but in terms of how well they respect or honor that value.[39] And this ranking will very plausibly have the **Disjunction Boundedness** property. If so, we will be able to appeal to these rankings in providing constraints on how non-promotional reasons can vary between sets of alternatives. To take just one example, if some fact $r$ explains why $A$ does a better job at respecting value $V$ than $B$ does, and why $B$ does better than $C$, it will likewise explain why $A$ does better than $C$. So we can see how the **Transitivity** constraint can be captured.[40]

So the assumption that all reasons involve promotion is not necessary for my purposes here. As long as we agree that some reasons involve promotion, my argument for contrastivism will go through. And, as I have pointed out, this puts pressure on us to adopt contrastivism about all reasons, even those that do not involve promotion. Finally, I have just shown how to capture the constraints on how reasons can vary for reasons that do not involve promotion.

---

[39] Some rankings will probably be pretty uninteresting, with one alternative at the top and all other alternatives tied at the bottom, as not respecting the value at all. For example, if I promise to $A$, then a ranking of the alternatives $\{A, B, C, D\}$ in terms of how well they respect the value of promise-keeping will be trivial in this way.

[40] It's possible that these non-promotional rankings will more often involve ties and incommensurability, since there are often plausibly different but equally or incommensurably good ways of respecting some value. This is no problem for the view I'm developing.

## 4.7 Where we Are

In this chapter, I've shown that an independent source of motivation for contrastivism—the relationship between reasons and promotion—leads very naturally to a version of the theory that straightforwardly solves an important problem for the contrastivist. By appealing to this idea, we can capture intuitive relationships between reasons relative to different sets of alternatives without sacrificing the independence that lets the contrastivist solve problems facing non-contrastive theories. Reasons relative to different sets of alternatives are independent of each other, but the theory also has an important kind of *structure*.

The theory I have developed here forms the heart of this book. In the next two chapters, I'll apply the theory to some important issues in ethics, practical reasoning, and epistemology. I'll show, first, that contrastivism allows us to frame important questions in new and interesting ways, and, second, that doing so lets us make some progress on them.

Before moving on, though, I want to take stock of where we are, in terms of the *depth* of contrastivism. In Chapter 3, I argued against a view I called *shallow contrastivism*, which holds that contrastivism goes only language-deep, and in favor of *deep contrastivism*, which holds that the important (possibly fundamental) normative reason—or favoring—relation is itself contrastive. Having developed the theory further in this chapter, however, we may wonder how deep contrastivism really goes. After all, the key to providing the constraints on how reasons can vary between sets of alternatives was to let things bottom out in a non-contrastive notion of promotion.

This is an important point. I think what the need for constraints, which I motivated at the beginning of this chapter, shows is that we cannot adopt an extremely deep form of contrastivism, at least not without incurring significant costs. So the theory I am endorsing is a somewhat *moderate* form of contrastivism. A deeper version would hold that there is no non-contrastive foundation: perhaps we can rank a given set of alternatives, but how actions are ranked against each other itself would vary if the relevant alternatives changed. For example, $A$ may be ranked higher than $B$ relative to a set $\{A, B, C\}$, but, once we introduce $D$, maybe $B$ would be ranked higher than $A$. Perhaps there are some arguments in favor of an extremely deep form of contrastivism like this, but I am not aware of any. And, given the significant costs this theory would take on—in particular, the cost of losing the relationships I've been discussing in this chapter—we would have to think hard about how strong such arguments were.

But, even though this theory is somewhat moderate, it is in opposition to nearly all existing work on reasons, which has traditionally assumed without argument that reasons are reasons for things *simpliciter*. Moreover, if the probabilistic view of promotion is true, and we can understand promotion in terms of conditional probabilities, then the non-contrastive foundation is not anything normative. (This may not be the case if we end up having to appeal to something like a ranking of alternatives in terms of how closely they approximate the ideal kind of honoring of some value.) So it may turn out that all the normative notions are contrastive, even if they bottom out in some non-contrastive, non-normative notion like conditional probability.

# 5
# Intransitivity

In Chapter 4, I developed a version of contrastivism (which we can call *moderate* contrastivism) that rules out a troubling kind of intransitivity of reasons, where *r* is a reason for *A* rather than *B* and for *B* rather than *C*, but not for *A* rather than *C*. This is an important result, because (i) contrastivism, described abstractly as the view that reasons are reasons only relative to sets of alternatives, initially seemed to allow for intransitivity, and (ii) this kind of intransitivity seems very implausible.

In this chapter, though, I introduce some pressure from the other direction: several writers have given powerful arguments that there really are cases of intransitivity in ethics and practical reasoning.[1] If they're correct—or even if we think they might be correct—a theory of reasons that simply rules out cases of intransitivity by definition looks problematic.

Importantly, from this perspective, an initial *attraction* of contrastivism, again described independently of the framework from Chapter 4, is that it seems better suited than non-contrastive theories to accommodate intransitivity. After all, a popular diagnosis of why intransitivity arises is that some moral factors are *essentially comparative*: whether or not a factor matters, or provides reasons, depends on the specific comparison being made.[2] If this thought is correct, then it seems that whether or not a fact is a reason for some action will depend on what you're comparing that action to, or the relevant set of alternative actions, since the factors or objectives that provide reasons do so only relative to some alternatives. And that is the central contrastivist claim. So the objection that we don't even *want* to rule out intransitivity is especially sharp for the contrastivist.

---

[1] See Temkin (1987, 1996, 2012), Rachels (1998, 2001), Friedman (2009).
[2] See in particular Temkin (1987, 1996, 2012).

The main thesis of this chapter is that the contrastivist theory I have developed can accommodate the kind of intransitivity for which Temkin, Rachels, and others have argued. But doing so is optional: it requires accepting a thesis that, though natural for a contrastivist, is far from obligatory. Isolating a particular thesis that generates intransitivity is useful for evaluating the plausibility (or implausibility) of intransitivity.

A more general goal of this chapter is to give some support to the claim that contrastivism lets us make progress in important debates in normative philosophy. I hope to have shown in the first four chapters of the book that the theory is independently well motivated. In this chapter and the next, I want to show that it's also theoretically useful. If I'm right that the view I develop in this chapter is a promising way to accommodate intransitivity, then we can use this view to frame important questions about that issue, since it will be a concrete example of a theory that allows for intransitivity. I want to emphasize right from the start, though, that it is not my goal to establish the possibility of intransitivity; in fact, I remain skeptical. Rather, I want to show that contrastivism sheds light on the debate, by showing us what kind of thesis we need to accept to accommodate intransitivity, if we want to do so, and by distinguishing it from similar but importantly distinct contrastivist claims.

## 5.1 Transitivity and Reasons

First I'll say a bit about what kind of intransitivity I'll be concerned with here. It is different from the sort that is most often discussed in the literature, but the two sorts are connected.

The most frequently discussed normative relation in the literature on intransitivity is the 'better than' relation.[3] Here is the principle at issue in those discussions:

**Transitivity of 'Better Than':** If $A$ is better than $B$, and $B$ is better than $C$, then $A$ is better than $C$.

For the purposes of this chapter, I'll treat the things that are ranked ($A$, $B$, and $C$) as outcomes or states of affairs. Arguments against this principle tend to describe cases (often bizarre, yet possible, cases) in which the

---

[3] See, e.g., Temkin (1987, 1996, 2012), Rachels (1998, 2001), Friedman (2009) for arguments in support of the intransitivity of 'better than'. Broome (1991) argues against this kind of intransitivity.

intuitive ranking of three (or more) states of affairs does not satisfy this principle. And frequently these arguments are based on cases devised by Parfit (1984), who does not, for what it's worth, think his cases show that 'better than' is intransitive. I'll present arguments in this vein in the next section.

Since I am concerned with reasons, I'll need to amend these arguments for the possibility of intransitivity of 'better than' to apply to reasons. Fortunately, this is easy to do, given the following linking principle:

**Reasons and Betterness:** *A* is better than *B* iff there is more reason to choose *A* than to choose *B*, given the choice between *A* and *B*.

This principle should be amenable both to those who want to analyze value in terms of reasons (e.g., Scanlon, 1998) and to those who want to analyze reasons in terms of value. Even if you don't think either of these analyses can succeed, the principle is very plausible.

Many writers have been attracted to *fitting-attitudes* accounts of value, on which to be good is just to be a fitting object of a pro-attitude, where fittingness is often, though not always, analyzed in terms of reasons.[4] **Reasons and Betterness** is attractive for some of the same reasons that these accounts are attractive. In particular, as many writers have pointed out, there are important connections between reasons and value. For example, if some outcome is valuable, then it is very plausible that there's a reason to choose that outcome, if given the choice. Of course, there might be stronger reasons to choose some other outcome, but, if that's so, then plausibly it is because the other outcome is more valuable—or better—in some way.[5] **Reasons and Betterness** predicts that there should be such a connection.

However, **Reasons and Betterness** does not require the truth of any fitting-attitudes account. We might instead take it as (part of) an analysis of reasons to choose in terms of value or betterness. Or we might think that there's some common third normative property that affects both the value and the strength of the reasons to choose the outcome. So, again, this principle is amenable to very different theories about the relationship between reasons and betterness.

---

[4] See Scanlon (1998), Rabinowicz and Rønnow-Rasmussen (2004), Suikkanen (2005, 2009), Danielsson and Olson (2007), Reisner (2009), Schroeder (2010), Way (2013) for a sampling of this literature.

[5] See, in particular, Way (2013) on this point.

The clause 'given the choice between A and B' is important here. That's because reasons to choose, like all reasons, are reasons *for agents*. But it is controversial whether the value of an outcome is similarly connected to agents. We might have two outcomes, A and B, such that A is intuitively better than B, even though no agent could have any reason to choose A because no agent could ever be in a position to make such a choice. The 'given the choice' clause blocks this. And moreover, in the cases I'll discuss, I'll simply stipulate that the agents involved face a choice between the relevant outcomes.

So, while arguments in the intransitivity literature present cases that challenge **Transitivity of 'Better Than'**, I'll make use of these cases in challenging the following principle:

**Transitivity of 'More Reason':** If there is more reason to choose A than to choose B, and more reason to choose B than to choose C, then there is more reason to choose A than to choose C.

I think this principle is *very* plausible, and that nearly everyone (except advocates of intransitivity that I mentioned above) would accept it, even independently of **Reasons and Betterness**.

Often these kinds of transitivity principles are simply taken for granted. Temkin (1987) hypothesizes that Parfit (1984) took it for granted that 'better than' (all-things-considered) is transitive, and that this influenced his reaction to the cases that I'll discuss in the next section. Broome (1991) claims that the transitivity of 'better than' is essentially a logical truth: "Whatever decisions we make, we shall always be guided by logic to preserve the transitivity of the comparative. [...] Logic requires betterness to be transitive."[6] The phrase 'more reason' suggests a view like this. It encourages us to think in terms of a linear scale, like the number line, so that to say that there is more reason to choose A than to choose B is like saying that choosing A falls to the right of choosing B on some line. And, once we have this picture in mind, it's easy to see why we would think that 'more reason' is transitive, since 'to the right of' is transitive. Nevertheless, I'll rehearse arguments in the next section that call these transitivity principles into question.

Before moving on, I should note one qualification. Some people think that two outcomes can be *incommensurable* in value—that the value of the

---

[6] Broome (1991: 12, 136).

two outcomes cannot be compared. If $A$ and $C$ are two such outcomes, it might be that $A$ is better than $B$ and $B$ is better than $C$ but not true that $A$ is better than $C$. This could hold if $B$ is commensurable with both $A$ and $C$, though $A$ and $C$ are incommensurable with one another. These kinds of cases, if they exist, are generally treated not as counterexamples to transitivity principles, but rather as exceptions. I could make this explicit by adding a clause to the principles like 'and $A$ and $C$ are commensurable', but I'll stick with the simpler formulation, and simply assume that all the outcomes I'm discussing are commensurable.

## 5.2 Intransitivity

The most popular kind of argument for the possibility of intransitivity is based on cases from Parfit (1984). Temkin (1987, 1996), Rachels (1998, 2001), and Friedman (2009) all give arguments based on Parfit's cases. These cases are an obvious place to begin because (i) denying the transitivity assumption is one way to avoid the problematic results, and (ii) other proposed solutions are unsatisfactory. That's not to say that many people find the solution of denying transitivity satisfactory, of course, but it does mean that we should at least give this solution a chance. The main argument I'll present here is essentially just what I think is the most compelling way to present the common thread from these other arguments. So I make no claim to originality.

First I'll show how one of Parfit's cases combined with **Transitivity of 'More Reason'** leads to what Parfit (1984) calls the *Repugnant Conclusion*. Parfit, and most other people, think this conclusion just can't be true. The common response is to reject a particular step in the argument other than the assumption of transitivity. But, as advocates of intransitivity have shown, this is shortsighted: there are big problems with this strategy, and, moreover, it leads us right back into a case—Parfit's *Mere Addition Paradox*—which calls **Transitivity of 'More Reason'** into question.

### 5.2.1 The Repugnant Conclusion

Consider the following case from Parfit (1984).[7] Suppose a powerful being asks you to choose between twenty-six states of the universe. Outcome

---

[7] See also Rachels (1998, 2001), Friedman (2009). As I have said, these authors are writing about 'better than (all things considered)', while I'm writing about 'more reason than'.

A[8] contains some relatively large population, say ten billion, all with a very high level of well-being. B contains a larger population—say for definiteness that it's twice as large as A—all with a lower, but still quite high, level of well-being. This reduced level of well-being is not due to any sort of unfairness or other moral deficiency—roughly, all the moral factors except for total and average utility are the same in the two outcomes. I think that, intuitively, there is more reason to choose B than to choose A. Agree with me for now, and I'll address worries about this first step below. Similarly, there is more reason to choose C than to choose B—it's twice as large, and everyone has only a slightly lower level of well-being. So by **Transitivity of 'More Reason'**, there is more reason to choose C than to choose A.

Continue this sequence until we get to Z. The population in Z is enormous—one billion times $2^{25}$. Everyone in Z has a level of well-being that makes their lives barely worth living ("muzak and potatoes," as Parfit would say). Well, there's more reason to choose B than to choose A, more reason to choose C than to choose B, more reason to choose D than to choose C, ..., more reason to choose Y than to choose X, and more reason to choose Z than to choose Y. So, if **Transitivity of 'More Reason'** is true, it follows that there's more reason to choose Z than to choose A. But this is what Parfit calls the *Repugnant Conclusion*: that for any outcome with a population of at least ten billion people, all of whom have unbelievably awesome lives, there is some possible outcome with a much larger population all of whose lives are barely worth living, such that there's more reason to choose this second outcome than the first.

This result seems wrong. But every step in the sequence seemed correct. As we move through the options in alphabetical order, there seemed to be more reason to choose each option than to choose the one before it.[9] If we

---

[8] Non-italicized capital letters are just names of outcomes that I've described. Italicized capital letters are variables ranging over outcomes.

[9] Rachels (1998) runs a similar argument by flipping the diagram upside down, and focusing on just one life for extremely long stretches of time. The idea is that, in outcome A, you face very intense pain for one year, while in B you face still intense, but slightly less intense, pain for one hundred years, and so on. In Z, you face very mild discomfort (with no redeeming qualities—you'd rather be temporarily unconscious, rather than experience the discomfort) for eons and eons. Each step—from A to B, from B to C, ..., from Y to Z—seems to be a step for the worse. So A is better than B is better than C ... is better than Y is better than Z. So if 'better than' is transitive, it follows that A is better than Z. But intuitively, Rachels thinks, Z is actually better than A—experiencing the very mild pain in Z, even for eons and eons, is not as bad as experiencing the most intense pain imaginable in A, even for only one year (make it 100 years and increase everything else accordingly,

want to retain both of these judgments—that the Repugnant Conclusion is false and that there's more reason to choose each option in the sequence than the one before it—it looks like we have to give up on **Transitivity of 'More Reason'**. That's the first argument for intransitivity.[10]

## 5.2.2 Resisting the first step

One way to block this argument, of course, is to resist one of the steps along the chain. I'll focus on the first step, from A to B, but I don't see why this choice should make a significant difference. Parfit himself thinks the Repugnant Conclusion forces us to deny that there is more reason to choose B than to choose A, because he assumes that transitivity holds.

This strategy seems to require us to say that there is in fact more reason to choose A than to choose B. If we said merely that there is *not* more reason to choose B than to choose A, then we should say, by parity of reasoning, that there's not more reason to choose C than to choose B, and so on. Then we could say that there's not more reason to choose Z than to choose A. But, if we don't say that there's more reason to choose A than to choose B, and so more reason to choose B than C, and so on, then transitivity-like considerations force us to say that there's not more reason to choose A than to choose Z. But this is also intuitively wrong—it isn't just that we think there's *not* more reason to choose Z than to choose A; we think there *is* more reason to choose A than to choose Z. The principle this argument relies on is the following.

> **Transitivity of 'Not More Reason':** If there's not more reason to choose A than to choose B, and not more reason to choose B than to choose C, then there cannot be more reason to choose A than to choose C.

And this is very similar to **Transitivity of 'More Reason'**.

---

if you aren't convinced). One potentially nice feature of this example, which I don't want to discuss here, is that arguably the reasons involved are all agent-relative reasons: since you're the one that's going to suffer the pain, they're reasons for you to choose the relevant option. Of course, if I was given the choice between which of these fates you would suffer, I would have agent-neutral reasons to choose the same options. But that's compatible with you having agent-relative reasons.

[10] Parfit (1984) considers and rejects several other kinds of responses, including an appeal to a *valueless level*: a level of well-being below which one's life doesn't contribute to the overall goodness of the outcome, or how much reason we would have to choose that outcome, though the life is still valuable to the one who lives it, since it is worth living. There are big problems with this view, as well as other attempts to avoid the Repugnant Conclusion.

Some writers who accept **Transitivity of 'More Reason'** would be willing to deny this last principle. Cases of incommensurability provide the most compelling counterexamples. Broome (1999) presents the following sort of case. Consider three possible careers: (i) a career as a lawyer, (ii) a career as a lawyer making $1,000 less per year, but that is otherwise identical to career (i), and (iii) a career as an academic. If the careers as a lawyer and career as an academic are sufficiently satisfying, it's plausible that you don't have more reason to choose career (i) than career (iii), or more reason to choose career (iii) than career (ii). The intuition here is that there a career as a lawyer and a career as an academic are simply valuable in different ways, so that neither is better than the other. And $1,000 per year is just not enough money to make a difference here. But, if all of this is right, it would follow from the **Transitivity of 'Not More Reason'** that you don't have more reason to choose career (i) than career (ii). But that's clearly false—since the two careers are otherwise identical, an extra $1,000 per year is exactly the kind of thing to give you more reason to choose (i) than to choose (ii). So there's some reason to think that this principle is false. This is far from uncontroversial, though.

But, even if we deny the **Transitivity of 'Not More Reason'** while retaining **Transitivity of 'More Reason'**, we could just make B contain many more people with levels of well-being barely below the level in A. And that sort of modification clearly gives us some additional reason to choose B. If there wasn't more reason to choose A than to choose B to begin with, it seems like this sort of modification should give us more reason to choose B than to choose A. That doesn't follow immediately, of course. But, if this sort of modification doesn't give us more reason to choose B than to choose A, we need some explanation for why.

So why think that there's more reason to choose A than to choose B? We're assuming that the outcomes are equivalent with respect to all the moral factors that they can be equivalent with respect to, while still exhibiting the relevant differences in total and average utility. So some moral factor with respect to which A is better than B must be making the difference, if there's more reason to choose A than to choose B. That is, the reasons provided by one of these moral factors must tip the scales in favor of A. The most obvious candidate is average utility.[11]

---

[11] See Temkin (1987) and Friedman (2009) for more thorough discussions of this sort of strategy.

Outcome A has a higher level of average utility than B, even though there's more total utility in B. If we want to appeal to average utility to resist the first step—to say that there's actually more reason to choose A than to choose B—we have to say that the difference in average utility is somehow more important than the difference in total utility. There are two ways to flesh out this response. First, we could say that average utility is one very important moral factor while admitting that total utility is also important, though less so, in determining what we have most reason to choose. Second, we could say that any increase in average utility is always better than any increase in total utility.

Suppose we take the first strategy. Then we admit that the fact that B has more total utility than A gives us some reason to choose B rather than A. But we just insist that the fact that A has higher average utility gives us *stronger reason* to choose A rather than B. Since A and B are identical with respect to other potentially relevant moral factors—we're assuming, for instance, that any violations of duties that take place in B are matched in A—we can thus deny that there's more reason to choose B than to choose A.[12] But as long as we admit that total utility gives us some reason to choose B rather than A, we can simply alter the case so that B has *much* more total utility than A and *very slightly* lower average utility. If we think total utility matters at all in this case, it's implausible that this sort of modification could never flip the scales, so that the vast increase in total utility finally outweighs the tiny increase in level of average well-being.

This pushes us toward the second strategy: no increase in total utility can make up for any deficiency in average utility. So, no matter how much more total utility B has, and no matter how small the difference in the level of average utility, there will always be more reason to choose A than to choose B. The problem with this strategy is that it's simply implausible. Consider a version of the case in which outcome A has just one person with a very high level of well-being, and outcome B has tens of billions of people all with this same level of well-being as the person in outcome A, plus a single person with a very slightly lower level of well-being. We can even imagine that this single person lives light years away from the

---

[12] Temkin (1987) considers the moral factor of *perfection*. See that paper for arguments that that sort of strategy fails. See that paper, as well as Friedman (2009), for more discussion of the objections I raise here.

others, so that he's not even aware of anyone with higher levels of well-being than himself.[13] The advocate of the second strategy has to hold that we still have more reason to choose outcome A than outcome B. And that is obviously implausible.

### 5.2.3 The Mere Addition Paradox

I've been arguing that we have more reason to choose B than to choose A, given the choice. And this sort of reasoning, along with **Transitivity of 'More Reason'**, leads to the Repugnant Conclusion. This gives us some reason to question this transitivity principle. But I haven't considered all the possible ways one might resist the first step of the argument (or some other step along the chain). So in this subsection I'm going to present an argument that, even if we find some way to resist the first step, and claim that there's more reason to choose A than to choose B, we *still* have reason to question **Transitivity of 'More Reason'**.[14]

The argument turns on Parfit's *Mere Addition Paradox* (1984). Parfit was forced to face this paradox by denying that B is better than A, in order to avoid the Repugnant Conclusion. For my purposes, of course, we face the version I'll present by denying that there's more reason to choose B than to choose A. Imagine an outcome A+ that contains all the same people as A, plus some additional people whose lives are well worth living, but whose levels of well-being are lower than that of the original group. But the two populations are totally unaware of one another. Imagine you are forced to choose between these three outcomes. Parfit argues that there is definitely not more reason to choose A than to choose A+—we cannot make an outcome worse by adding happy people to it. There is a drop in equality and in average well-being, but we haven't introduced any inequality via any sort of injustice. This sort of addition is what Parfit calls *mere addition*, and he claims that mere addition can never make an outcome worse. So we don't have more reason to choose A than to choose A+.[15]

A+ contains just as many people as B. Parfit argues that there's more reason to choose B than A+: I stipulate that B is better with respect to equality, total well-being, and average well-being. Thus, it's hard to see

---

[13] Compare Parfit's Mere Addition Paradox (1984); more on this later.

[14] See Friedman (2009).

[15] I think that we plausibly have more reason to choose A+ than to choose A. Parfit denies this. But nothing really turns on this for my purposes here.

what would motivate us to think there's more reason to choose A+ than to choose B.

But remember that we're assuming that there's more reason to choose A than to choose B, in order to avoid the Repugnant Conclusion while retaining **Transitivity of 'More Reason'**. Note again that it's not easy to see how to avoid the Repugnant Conclusion if we say merely that there's not more reason to choose B than to choose A—we could just double the size of B and make the level of well-being of its inhabitants even closer to the level of the inhabitants of A. But, if there's more reason to choose A than to choose B, and more reason to choose B than to choose A+, then it follows from **Transitivity of 'More Reason'** that there's more reason to choose A than to choose A+. But Parfit argued, and it seems very plausible that, this is actually false. This is the Mere Addition Paradox. And we got ourselves into it by claiming that there's more reason to choose A than to choose B—that is, by resisting the first step of the argument for the Repugnant Conclusion. And we could give a version of the Mere Addition Paradox for any adjacent members of the chain (for F and G, rather than for A and B, say). So, once we try to avoid the Repugnant Conclusion, we walk right into the Mere Addition Paradox, which *also* gives us reason to question **Transitivity of 'More Reason'**.

## 5.3 Intransitivity and Contrastivism

I've argued that Parfit's cases give us reason to question **Transitivity of 'More Reason'**. I've considered some ways to resist the argument, and shown that they either lead to implausible results or else lead us right back to problems for transitivity. So we should take seriously the idea that 'more reason than' is intransitive.

This puts some pressure on the version of contrastivism I developed in Chapter 4, which seems to simply rule out intransitivity by definition. This is even more striking, given that an initial attraction of a contrastive theory of reasons might be that it seems better placed to deny **Transitivity of 'More Reason'**. The idea that reasons relative to different sets of alternatives are independent of one another—that settling what the reasons are relative to one set does not tell us what the reasons are relative to a different set—might make us think contrastivism is well placed to accommodate intransitivity. That's because, as I emphasized in Chapter

4, transitivity seems to amount to a constraint on this independence. But I showed that the framework I developed there actually *does* constrain this independence. It cannot turn out, according to that framework, that *r* is a reason for *A* rather than *B* and for *B* rather than *C*, but not a reason for *A* rather than *C*. So, if the arguments for intransitivity are at least compelling enough that we don't want to rule it out by definition, there seems to be a problem for the view I developed in the previous chapter.

### 5.3.1 Two kinds of intransitivity

To start to see why this is not actually a problem, I'll distinguish between two kinds of intransitivity. I'll first show that the sort of intransitivity that the view from Chapter 4 rules out is not the sort that the arguments from the previous section purport to establish.

First, we might have what I'll call *intransitivity of reasons*. If this sort of intransitivity is possible, then there might be a case in which some fact *r* is a reason for *A* rather than *B* and for *B* rather than *C*, but not a reason for *A* rather than *C*. Recall that, in Chapter 4, I pointed out that the intuitive transitivity requirement on reasons is even stronger, once we think of reasons in terms of promotion. It isn't just that whenever *r* is a reason for *A* rather than *B* and for *B* rather than *C*, it must be a reason for *A* rather than *C*. The objective (whatever fills in for '*O*' in the principles **For** and **Against**) that explains why *r* is a reason for *A* rather than *B* and for *B* rather than *C* (if there is a common objective that explains both of these things) must also explain why *r* is a reason for *A* rather than *C*. The intuition behind a transitivity requirement wouldn't really be captured if *something else* explained why *r* is a reason for *A* rather than *C*. This is the variety of intransitivity that the framework from Chapter 4 straightforwardly rules out.

Second, we might have what I'll call *intransitivity of 'more reason'*. If this sort of intransitivity is possible, then there might be a case in which there is *more reason* for *A* than for *B* and more reason for *B* than for *C*, but not more reason for *A* than for *C*.

The arguments for intransitivity from the previous section, if they're successful, establish only the intransitivity of 'more reason'. What seems wrong is that there's *more reason* to choose outcome Z than to choose outcome A. But it is not counterintuitive to say that there is *some reason* to choose outcome Z rather than outcome A. In particular, considerations of total utility provide a reason to choose outcome Z rather than outcome A. The fact that, say, more utility is better than less is a reason to choose B rather than A, a reason to choose C rather than B, ..., and a reason to choose Z rather than Y. It follows from the transitivity of reasons that it's a reason to choose Z rather than A. And this seems correct. It's just that the reason is outweighed by the reasons to choose A rather than choose Z, explained or provided by some other factor, like average utility.

If this is right, then it's not simply that the cases don't support the intransitivity of reasons. They actually offer strong support—at least rhetorically—for the *transitivity* of reasons. If this is the most compelling support for intransitivity—and the fact that advocates of intransitivity almost invariably appeal to these cases is some evidence for this—and it seems *wrong* to describe them as cases of intransitivity of reasons, that casts serious doubt on this kind of intransitivity.

## 5.4 Contrast-Sensitive Importance

Even once we recognize the difference between these two types of intransitivity, it's still a bit mysterious how we could have intransitivity of 'more reason' without the intransitivity of reasons. In this section I'll show how to pry them apart. I'll offer a way of accommodating the intransitivity of 'more reason' in the framework from Chapter 4, even though it clearly rules out the intransitivity of reasons. I'll take this in two steps. First I'll observe that the strength of reasons depends on the importance of the objectives (desires, values, and so on) that provide those reasons. Then I'll suggest that the importance of a given objective might *itself* be a contrast-sensitive matter: an objective that matters a lot in making some comparisons might matter very little in making other comparisons. So the resulting view is that, even if a fact is a reason for some action relative to both of two different sets of alternatives, it might be a much weightier reason relative to one of them, owing to the contrast-sensitivity of the importance of the objective that provides that reason.

### 5.4.1 Strength of reasons and importance of objectives

I argued in the previous section that Parfit's cases don't push us towards the intransitivity of reasons, but only towards the intransitivity of 'more reason'. But this seems unstable. The intransitivity of reasons appears to be necessary for the intransitivity of 'more reason'. After all, if any fact that's a reason for A rather than B and for B rather than C is thereby a reason for A rather than C, the combined strength of the reasons would also seem to be transitive. Thus, it seems that, since the view from Chapter 4 rules out the intransitivity of reasons, it also rules out the intransitivity of 'more reason than'.

But in fact the intransitivity of 'more reason than' does not require the intransitivity of reasons. An important first step is recognizing that the combined strength or weight of the reasons for A doesn't depend only, or even most importantly, on *how many* reasons there are. Frequently there are more reasons to do A than to do B, but stronger there is reason to do B. The fact that I'd get my shoes muddy is a reason not to run into the pond to save the drowning child, as is the fact that I would be late for the movie. The fact that the child will die if I don't is a reason to save him. So that's two reasons not to save and only one reason to save. But clearly the reason to save is stronger than the combined strength of the reasons not to save. And the explanation for this is that the objective that explains why I have this reason—saving the child's life—is much more *important* than the objectives that explain why I have the reasons not to save—keeping my shoes clean and seeing the movie. So how much reason there is to perform an action depends—in large part, at least—on the importance of the objectives that provide those reasons.

An important upshot of this observation is that we cannot simply read off how strong a particular reason to A is, or what the combined strength of the reasons to A is, from the rankings (perhaps provided by conditional probabilities) that I used in Chapter 4. We need some account of the relative importance of the various reason-providing objectives. I don't have an account of this, but there are intuitively clear cases, like the one I mentioned involving the drowning child.[16]

---

[16] It doesn't follow, though, that the facts about rankings are irrelevant. First, and most importantly for my purposes, the rankings establish what reasons there are, relative to a given set of alternatives. This is very important, because it lets us retain the nice entailment relations I established in Chapter 4. I'll have a bit more to say about this shortly. Second, facts about rankings can arguably make a difference when the objectives that provide two reasons are equally important. Suppose objectives $X$ and $Y$ are equally important, but that the degree to which $A$-ing promotes $X$ is greater than the degree to which $B$-ing promotes $Y$. Then plausibly the reasons that $X$ provides for $A$ are stronger than the reasons that $Y$ provides for $B$.

## 5.4.2 Contrast-sensitive importance

It's still not clear, though, how to allow for the intransitivity of 'more reason' once we rule out the intransitivity of reasons. Even if the strength of an $O$-provided reason for $A$ out of $\{A, B\}$ and for $B$ out of $\{B, C\}$ depends on the importance of $O$, the strength of the $O$-provided reason to $A$ out of $\{A, C\}$ will likewise depend on the importance of $O$. And, if $O$ is very important, then it's going to provide relatively strong reasons across all of these sets of alternatives. So the transitivity of 'more reason' still seems to follow from the transitivity of reasons. For example, the objective of saving an innocent life is very important. Assume that this objective provides reasons to do $A$ rather than $B$ and $B$ rather than $C$. These will, of course, be weighty reasons. Well, by the transitivity of reasons, it will also provide reasons to do $A$ rather than $C$. But, again, this objective is very important. So it looks as if these reasons will also be very weighty.

To see that this is wrong, it might be instructive first to see how we could allow for the intransitivity of reasons while retaining (something like) the framework from Chapter 4. What we would have to do is to let the objectives that provide reasons vary with sets of alternatives. If $O$ provides reasons relative to $\{A, B\}$ and $\{B, C\}$, but not relative to $\{A, C\}$, then we could have cases of intransitivity of reasons. This would be to adopt an even deeper form of contrastivism than the version I developed in the previous chapter, since we would no longer ultimately explain reasons in terms of some non-contrastive base. The most important cost to adopting this kind of picture, though, is that we would lose the entailment relations between reasons relative to different, but related, sets that I established in Chapter 4. Even if we are convinced that the transitivity requirement is questionable, the other entailments involving subsets, supersets, and so on are very attractive. So we should try to retain them if possible.[17]

The framework from Chapter 4 delivered relations between what reasons there are relative to different sets. Changing what objectives can provide reasons between sets of alternatives leads to a difference in these facts. So, to retain the entailment relations, we need to hold the objectives fixed between sets of alternatives. No matter what the relevant set

---

[17] One way to try to retain these entailment relations on this more radical picture would be to place some restrictions on how the reason-providing objectives could vary between sets of alternatives. I won't explore this option here, since, as I have argued, the arguments for intransitivity don't even purport to establish intransitivity of reasons.

of alternatives is, there is one class of objectives that provide reasons, though they'll provide reasons for different things relative to different sets of alternatives, of course, depending on which alternatives in the set best promote them.

But, as I have argued, the *strength* of the reasons for some action depends on more than what reasons there are: it depends on the importance of the objectives that provide those reasons. So the way to accommodate the intransitivity of 'more reason' while retaining the transitivity of reasons (and the other entailment relations) is to let the relative importance of the objectives vary between sets of alternatives. Some objective O *always* gives us reasons, but these reasons are more or less weighty, depending on the set of alternatives, since the importance of the objectives varies with sets of alternatives.[18] Thus, even if every fact that is a reason for A rather than B and for B rather than C is thereby a reason for A rather than C, the weights of these reasons may vary depending on the comparison. We might have some very weighty reasons for A rather than B and for B rather than C that are much weaker reasons for A rather than C, because the relative importance of the objectives that provide these reasons varies with specific comparisons being made. Then we can fail to have more reason for A than for C without giving up on the transitivity of reasons.

This is a way of spelling out the intuition, often appealed to in the anti-transitivity literature, that some values or objectives are essentially comparative.[19] Differences with respect to some value such as equality, total utility, or average utility might make a big difference when comparing some alternatives, but matter much less when comparing other alternatives. We can allow that having more total utility, for example, is always a reason to choose an outcome rather than choosing one with less total utility. But, depending on other features of the alternatives, this reason can be stronger or weaker. And that's because considerations of total utility might be more or less important depending on the comparison.

---

[18] If there are some cases—though I haven't seen any—that do seem to establish the intransitivity of reasons, we could even accommodate that, or something like it, on this picture. We would just let some objectives provide reasons of *no weight*, relative to some sets of alternatives. So it would still be true to say that the fact is a reason, and we could retain the entailment relations. It's just that the reasons have no weight.

[19] See especially Temkin (1987, 1996, 2012). See also Rachels (2001: 218): "a factor determining how A&Z compare differs dramatically in significance from how it figures in comparing A&B, B&C, C&D, and so on."

Here's an illustrative and particularly relevant example. When comparing two outcomes with relatively close levels of average utility, like any two adjacent outcomes in the sequence I used in the argument for the Repugnant Conclusion, total utility may be more important than average utility. That would explain why, when comparing any two adjacent outcomes, there's always more reason to choose the one later in the sequence—more reason to choose G than to choose F out of {choose F, choose G}, for example. But, when we have vast differences in average utility, total utility may be much less important than average utility. If that's right, it would explain why there's more reason to choose A than to choose Z, even though there's so much more total utility in Z. Even though considerations of total utility do provide a reason to choose Z out of {choose A, choose Z}, this reason may be much weaker than the reason to choose A provided by average utility. That would explain why there's more reason to choose A than to choose Z out of {choose A, choose Z}. On the other hand, the reason provided by average utility to choose A out of {choose A, choose B} might be weaker than the reason provided by total utility to choose B out of this set—that would explain why there's more reason to choose B. The importance of total utility depends (probably among other things) on the relative levels of average utility, and vice versa. The simplistic idea here is just that the importance of an objective may vary along with the difference in the degree to which that objective is instantiated by the relevant alternatives. But there may be other features of the alternatives in a set that determine how important a given objective is, relative to that set.

Let me emphasize again that I do not mean to commit myself to this particular kind of variation in importance, or indeed to any kind of variation in importance. This is just an illustration of the kind of picture we may want to adopt, if we find the arguments for intransitivity convincing.

### 5.4.3 Contrastivism about reasons and importance

Contrastivism about reasons is the view that whether or not some consideration is a reason for an action or attitude depends on the alternatives. The strategy for accommodating the intransitivity of 'more reason' that I've just outlined involves making the importance of reason-providing objectives, and thus the strength of reasons, depend on the alternatives. What is the relationship between these two ideas?

First, we can be contrastivists about reasons without adopting a contrast-sensitive view of the importance of objectives. That is, the strategy I've outlined in this section is *detachable* from the rest of the contrastivist theory I've developed in previous chapters. So, if you do not find the arguments for intransitivity compelling, or just find the difficulties that come along with intransitivity (some of which I'll discuss in the next section) too troubling, that's no reason not to be a contrastivist. You can just hold the importance of objectives fixed across sets of alternatives to rule out intransitivity.

Second, we can adopt a contrast-sensitive view of the importance of objectives without being contrastivists about reasons. On this kind of view, whether or not some fact is a reason for A does not depend on the alternatives, though the weight of that reason does depend on the alternatives. For example, the total utility in Z always provides a reason to choose Z (*simpliciter*, of course). But, when we compare choosing Z to choosing A, that reason is simply not very weighty, though it is quite weighty when we compare choosing Z with choosing Y. Note that this is precisely what the contrastivist says about these particular comparisons. The difference between the two views will be the following. The non-contrastivist about reasons says that the total utility in A provides a reason to choose A even when we compare it to choosing Z. But the contrastivist denies this: total utility doesn't provide any reason to choose A when we compare it with choosing Z (or, as the contrastivist would rather say, no reason to choose A *rather than* choose Z), since Z has more total utility than A. But the important point for now is that the non-contrastivist about reasons can still be a contrastivist about importance, and accommodate intransitivity in the way I've suggested here.

It's worth pointing out, though, that accepting contrast-sensitive importance is a particularly natural thing for a contrastivist to do. The contrastivist about reasons is impressed by the role that relevant alternatives seem to have in our judgments about what is a reason for what. So thinking that alternatives can also matter for *how strong* those reasons are is right up the contrastivist's alley.

Other writers—particularly Temkin—have emphasized that intransitivity is generated by essentially comparative values or objectives. Approaching this issue from a contrastivist perspective has allowed us to isolate this thesis, and to distinguish it from other theses. The claim that generates intransitivity is that reason-providing objectives may have contrast-sensitive importance—this is the sense in which they are essentially comparative. Crucially, though, this is not to say that either what reasons there are, or the objectives that provide them, must vary with the contrasts. In fact, I have argued that the standard arguments for intransitivity do not even support these claims. What we do not need to do, and probably do not even want to do, is say that some objectives or factors simply do not provide reasons at all for some comparisons. This would lead to the intransitivity of reasons, and we have not found any support for that thesis.

What we need is some explanation for why the reason-providing objectives should vary in importance across comparisons, in the ways required by the arguments for intransitivity. The discussion in this chapter has been almost entirely abstract and formal—I've simply tried to make room for this kind of view, and to say in abstract terms what kinds of commitments it takes on. The substantive work for an advocate of intransitivity, then, is to explain contrast-sensitive importance. This may involve interesting discussion of the interaction between different objectives. For example, the relative average utility of two outcomes may make a difference in the importance of total utility, when comparing those outcomes. Questions about how and why this happens are interesting and important. But I will not attempt to enter into this discussion here.

## 5.5 Remaining Questions

In this section I'll discuss two remaining issues for the view I've developed here. Throughout the discussion, I'll flag issues that would need to be resolved before we should feel comfortable adopting the account in this chapter. Thus, the upshot of this discussion isn't that this account is the correct one. It's rather that it offers a plausible *start*, if we want to accommodate intransitivity.

### 5.5.1 What should I do?

An important question for any theory that allows for intransitivity of 'more reason' concerns how we should decide what to do. A natural view is that you should do what you have most reason to do. But consider the imagined choice you face in the Repugnant Conclusion case: {choose A, choose B, . . . , choose Z}. What out of this set do you have most reason to do? In Chapter 3, I adopted CRO, which says that we have to look at the two-member subsets: the option you should take out of the larger set is the one that wins in all of its pairwise comparisons.

So suppose we know what to say for any two-member subset of this larger set.[20] Well, part of the point of this case was that *nothing* wins in all of the pairwise comparisons. And this is the result that the account I have developed here gives. So the account I've offered so far doesn't tell us what to do in this case; in fact, it tells us that there is nothing that we ought to do in this case—at least, none of the options in the set {choose A, choose B, …, choose Z}. And a theory of reasons, we might hope, will tell us what to do, once we know the facts about the reasons and their weights. After all, what we should do is intuitively determined by our reasons.

But, if we accept intransitivity, then our theory should *not* tell us that we should perform some particular alternative out of the larger set in this case. That's just because any answer the theory gives will seem intuitively wrong. If the theory gave us some answer here, there are two possibilities. First, it might say that we should choose Z. Well, that seems wrong, since there's more reason to choose A. Second, it might say that we should choose some outcome besides Z. That also seems wrong, though, since there's intuitively more reason to perform the next outcome in the sequence. So I take it that it's actually a *virtue* of the account that it doesn't deliver an (inevitably unsatisfying) answer as to what we should do in a case of intransitivity.

Contrastivism (plus contrast-sensitive importance) gets all of the pairwise cases for adjacent alternatives, which we do have strong intuitions about, correct. But we don't have strong intuitions about pairwise comparisons between non-adjacent alternatives. For example, what is there most reason to do out of {choose D, choose P}? It's hard to say. This is going to depend on whether we think the additional total utility in P provides a strong enough reason to choose P to outweigh the reason provided by the higher average utility in D. These are hard questions, but I won't address them here.

So the view developed in this chapter gives the correct results in cases that we have strong intuitions about, and tells us exactly how to decide in pairwise cases we don't have strong intuitions about—we just have to compare the weights of the reasons provided by the various factors. A disadvantage is that, since the weights of these reasons can vary widely

---

[20] This doesn't actually seem true to me—what should we say about {choose A, choose N}? More on this shortly. The important point, though, is that we do know what to say about any adjacent pair, and about {choose A, choose Z}.

depending on the comparison being made, there doesn't seem to be a neat, systematic way to do that. A theory that did not allow the weight of the reasons to vary—or at least made them vary in a systematic way—would be neater, but I don't see how to give such a theory while still capturing the intuitively clear cases. This is an important open issue. If there's no good way to make progress on it, then we should be wary of accepting this account.

### 5.5.2 Why so uncommon?

The second issue I want to consider is the following. Even if we think intransitivity is theoretically possible, and so want a theory that can accommodate it, it's plausibly a desideratum on any theory that allows for intransitivity to give some explanation for why intransitivity is so rare. After all, the cases that are most often appealed to as alleged examples of intransitivity are Parfit's cases, which I have already described. And these are extraordinary cases, to say the least. In any ordinary case, transitivity seems to hold. But, if there's no formal obstacle to intransitivity, it looks as though every single situation any real person will ever face is just a special case. On the theory I've suggested here, in particular, cases in which transitivity holds look like *very* special cases. The importance of the reason-providing objectives across different sets of alternatives just happens to work out conveniently. We need some explanation of this. If we can't offer such an explanation, then we should be very skeptical that the theory I've offered here is correct.[21]

To satisfy this desideratum, we would need to give an explanation of why intransitivity will be rare, even though there's no formal obstacle. I don't see how to adjust the structural features of the account to give such an explanation. So the strategy has to be to appeal to substantive facts about particular cases. As long as the substantive facts that generate intransitivity are rare enough, we can get the explanation we want.

The crucial feature of the account is what I called contrast-sensitive importance of objectives. That's the feature that lets the weight of reasons

---

[21] It's worth reiterating here that the official view of this book is the one developed in Chapter 4. So, if you find intransitivity too problematic, you can simply reject the amendment under discussion in this chapter—namely, tacking on contrast-sensitive importance of reason-providing objectives.

vary with sets of alternatives. So, if the importance of objectives only varies—or only varies *significantly*—when extraordinary sets of alternatives are involved, we could explain why intransitivity is so rare. If, relative to all the sets of alternatives that are ordinarily relevant, the importance of a given objective is relatively constant, we won't get intransitivity in ordinary cases. But we can still get intransitivity when we compare the strength of reasons between ordinary and extraordinary cases, or among extraordinary cases.

Consider the sequence of outcomes from the argument for the Repugnant Conclusion. Now, any given set of alternatives consisting of choosing members of this sequence isn't really *ordinary*. But what is ordinary about sets like {choose A, choose B} or {choose Y, choose Z} is that we're choosing between outcomes in which the average levels of utility are relatively close. Usually when we choose between some alternatives, our choice won't make a drastic change in the average level of utility, at least not while leading to an increase in the total amount of utility. Of course, some people may face choices between one outcome and another that would lead to a much lower average level of utility for some part of the population. But the second choice will generally lead to a much lower total level of utility, as well.

So here is a suggestion on behalf of the supporter of intransitivity. The importance of the objectives of total utility and average utility remains relatively stable between sets like {choose A, choose B} and {choose A, choose C}. It's only when we consider a set like {choose A, choose Z} that the importance of the objectives can shift significantly. So the intransitivity of 'more reason' is going to arise only when some of the sets we're considering are extraordinary—in particular, when there are drastic differences in the average level of utility between the outcomes. That explains why intransitivity is so rare: we don't generally consider extraordinary sets of alternatives.

I have already said that the substantive work for an advocate of intransitivity is to explain contrast-sensitive importance, perhaps by appealing to interactions between objectives. For example, relative levels of average utility may influence the importance of total utility. The idea that the importance of some objectives remains stable across ordinary comparisons may be one constraint on a theory of these interactions. So I do not claim to have provided an answer to the question of why intransitivity is so rare; instead, keeping with the abstract character of this chapter,

I have tried to describe some features that an acceptable answer would have to have.

Some explanation along these lines has to work, if the theory I have developed in this chapter is going to be acceptable. I think the prospects of developing this explanation into something plausible are promising. But it would obviously take more work than what I've done here. All I want to suggest is that the package I've developed in this chapter is one very promising way to begin accommodating intransitivity.

## 5.6 Conclusion

In Chapter 4, I developed a contrastivist view of reasons, and showed that it rules out a certain kind of troubling intransitivity. In this chapter, I have considered an objection from the other direction: intransitivity actually is possible, and, moreover, an initial attraction of contrastivism—ignoring the framework from Chapter 4—is that it seems especially well placed to accommodate it. I have argued that the sort of intransitivity that this objector has in mind actually is compatible with, though not required by, the framework from Chapter 4, and shown how to accommodate it. I want to remain neutral on whether intransitivity is possible; all I meant to do in this chapter was demonstrate that contrastivism can accommodate it.

Another more general goal of this chapter was to show that the view I developed in the first four chapters of the book provides an interesting way to think about important debates in ethics and practical reasoning. We can reframe these debates in contrastivist terms and make progress by exploiting the extra resources that contrastivism gives us. In this chapter, I hope to have shown that appealing to natural contrastivist ideas—in particular, contrast-sensitive importance of reason-providing objectives—lets us make some progress in the debate over the possibility of intransitivity. In the next chapter, I'll apply the theory to an interesting issue from epistemology, and an analogous issue in practical reasoning: the rationality of *withholding* belief, on one hand, and intention, on the other.

# 6

# Withholding

In the first four chapters of this book, I developed and defended contrastivism about reasons. My goal now is to show that this theory has some interesting applications in different areas of normative philosophy. In the previous chapter I showed how contrastivism lets us make progress in the debate over the possibility of the intransitivity of 'more reason than'. In this chapter, I turn to an application from theoretical and practical rationality. An important, but often neglected, issue from these domains is the rationality of *withholding* an attitude—belief, in the theoretical case, and intention, in the practical case. Sometimes the most rational thing to do is neither to believe that $p$ nor to believe that $\neg p$, but *not to make up your mind* with respect to $p$, or *to withhold* belief. Similarly, sometimes it's more rational to withhold intention with respect to $\phi$, rather than intend to $\phi$ or intend not to $\phi$.[1]

In this chapter I will develop an account of when an agent ought to withhold, which applies to both belief and intention, which follows very naturally from the contrastive account of reasons I have developed. This account has several attractive explanatory features, and avoids problems that face an initially attractive non-contrastive account of when agents ought to withhold.

---

[1] Throughout the book, I have been using italicized uppercase letters from the Roman alphabet as variables for both actions and attitudes. In this chapter, I will use Greek letters as variables for actions, primarily as the contents of intentions (or the withholding of intentions). I will follow standard convention and use lowercase letters as variables for propositions, primarily as the contents of beliefs (or the withholding of beliefs).

## 6.1 Withholding Belief and Contrastive Reasons

I will develop the account for the epistemic case of withholding belief first, and then extend it to the practical case of withholding intention.

Since we are trying to provide an account of what doxastic attitude you *ought* to have, and what you ought to do depends on your reasons, we need to figure out what your reasons are in this kind of case. Given the contrastive theory of reasons I've developed, we need to look at your reasons relative to some set of alternatives or other. If we are trying to decide what doxastic attitude you should take towards $p$, the most natural set of alternatives is {believe $p$, believe $\neg p$, withhold belief with respect to $p$}.[2] That is, the relevant alternatives will be believing that $p$ is true, believing that $p$ is false (or *disbelieving p*), and not making up your mind one way or the other.

I have just said that believing, disbelieving, and withholding are alternatives. Throughout this book, I have been assuming or stipulating that the members of a set of alternatives are mutually exclusive. This is easy to do when the alternatives are actions—I can simply stipulate that performing one alternative precludes performing the others. Things are trickier here, since it is possible for agents to hold more than one of these doxastic attitudes. This is especially clear in the case of belief and disbelief, where disbelieving $p$ is simply believing $\neg p$. Such an agent would have contradictory, and probably irrational (though this is controversial), beliefs. But it does seem possible. So the kind of mutual exclusivity at issue cannot be anything as strong as logical, metaphysical, or even psychological incompatibility. I will instead assume that these states are *rationally* incompatible: if the agent is rational, she will not have more than one of them. If agents can rationally have contradictory beliefs—perhaps in Frege's Puzzle cases—things will have to be more complicated. But I will have to set this issue aside.

One initially plausible deflationary view about withholding belief is that it is reducible to not believing and not disbelieving. But I will assume throughout this chapter that withholding belief with respect to $p$ is a distinct kind of attitude, not equivalent to merely not believing $p$ and not disbelieving $p$. Some prima facie evidence for this claim is that there

---

[2] I will ignore more fine-grained attitudes, like credences, here.

seems to be an important difference between an agent who has considered a proposition, and still neither believes it nor disbelieves it, and an agent who has not even considered the proposition, and therefore neither believes it nor disbelieves it. So I will be treating withholding belief as itself a kind of committed attitude.[3] I will make the same kind of assumption about withholding intention—namely, that it is not merely failing to intend to $\phi$ and failing to intend not to $\phi$.

Recall the principle relating what an agent ought to do with her contrastive reasons that I have adopted:

**CRO:** $s$ ought to $A$ out of $Q$ iff $s$ has most reason to $A$ out of $\{A, B\}$, for all of the other alternatives $B$ in $Q$.

When $A$-ing wins in the pairwise comparisons with each of the other alternatives, you ought to $A$. Now we can just straightforwardly apply this to belief:

**O(Bel)*:** $s$ ought to believe $p$ out of {believe $p$, believe $\neg p$, withhold} iff $s$ has most reason to believe $p$ out of {believe $p$, believe $\neg p$} and $s$ has most reason to believe $p$ out of {believe $p$, withhold}.

This principle is very plausible: you ought to believe $p$ just in case you have better reason to do so than either to disbelieve $p$ or to withhold belief. More importantly for the purposes of this chapter, CRO gives us the following account of when an agent ought to withhold belief:

**O(Wh-B)*:** $s$ ought to withhold belief in $p$ out of {believe $p$, believe $\neg p$, withhold} iff $s$ has most reason to withhold belief in $p$ out of {believe $p$, withhold} and $s$ has most reason to withhold out of {believe $\neg p$, withhold}.

This principle, like O(Bel)*, is just the one that follows straightforwardly from the theory I've developed so far.

### 6.1.1 Contrastive epistemic reasons

So in providing an account of when an agent ought to withhold belief, we need to look at four kinds of reasons: (i) reasons to withhold rather than believe $p$, (ii) reasons to believe $p$ rather than withhold, (iii) reasons

---

[3] See, e.g., Sturgeon (2010), Friedman (2013a, b).

to withhold rather than believe ¬p, and (iv) reasons to believe ¬p rather than withhold. Since we want to figure out what doxastic attitude an agent ought to take towards p, it is also important to have an account of (v) reasons to believe p rather than believe ¬p and (vi) reasons to believe ¬p rather than believe p. What we need next, then, is some account of what these reasons are, so that we know what to compare.

Before providing that account, though, I need to make an important clarification. I said above that I am giving a view of what doxastic attitude an agent ought to take toward a proposition, and, more specifically, when an agent ought to withhold belief in a proposition. The 'ought' here should be read in a particular way, as the 'ought' of *epistemic rationality*. So, I will provide an account of when you ought, *epistemically*, to withhold belief in a proposition. This epistemic 'ought' is the one at work in the most natural interpretation of claims such as 'You ought to believe what your evidence supports' or 'You ought not to believe contradictions'. Similarly, the reasons I will be talking about are *epistemic* reasons—reasons that bear on what you epistemically ought to do.[4]

The most useful way to characterize epistemic reasons for my purposes here is by distinguishing them from non-epistemic reasons to believe a proposition or withhold belief in a proposition. If a powerful demon threatens to kill you if you believe that there is a glass on the table, that is a (very strong!) reason not to believe that there is a glass on the table.[5] But this reason is importantly different from the reasons provided by evidence that there is a glass on the table, like the fact that you seem to see a glass on the table. The fact that you seem to see a glass on the table is a reason to believe that there is a glass on the table.[6] This is a paradigm example of an epistemic reason—assuming that you don't have any other evidence that there is not a glass on the table, or any reasons to disregard your visual evidence, the epistemically rational thing for you to do is believe

---

[4] Two clarifications: (i) I do not mean to claim that 'ought' is ambiguous, in any deep sense, between this use and a practical use; for all I have said, the difference can be traced to contextual elements, like Kratzer's ordering source and modal base (1981). (ii) There is another use of 'epistemic ought' that differs from my use in this paragraph; this is sometimes also called the *predictive* use, and it is at work in the most natural interpretation of 'The roast ought to be done by now'.

[5] For discussion of this *wrong kind of reasons* problem, see, for a small sampling, D'Arms and Jacobson (2000a, b), Rabinowicz and Rønnow-Rasmussen (2004), Schroeder (2012b). Pascal's Wager provides another classic example of a practical reason for belief.

[6] I am glossing over issues about perceptual justification and evidence here.

that there is a glass on the table. But this may not be the *practically* rational thing to do in this case. In this practical sense, plausibly, you ought not to believe that there is a glass on the table, since the demon's threat gives you very strong practical—but not epistemic—reason not to believe this. The demon's reason does not bear on what it is epistemically rational for you to do, though it does bear on what it is practically rational for you to do. There is a huge literature on these issues. But in my discussion of belief and withholding belief in this chapter, I will ignore them, and stipulate that I am talking only about epistemic reasons.

One final point before I move on to give a contrastivist account of epistemic reasons. This last example may tempt you to think that epistemic reasons are all evidence for or against the proposition, while non-epistemic reasons involve good or bad features of being in the doxastic state (belief, disbelief, or withholding) itself. In fact lots of people have been tempted to exactly this kind of view.[7] But, as Schroeder (2012b) argues, there are epistemic reasons besides evidence. For example, the fact that you have very little information and expect to get more soon is intuitively an epistemic reason to withhold belief. It bears on what doxastic attitude it is rational for you to have—in this case, withholding belief. This is, not surprisingly, a very important point for this chapter, since I will be talking mostly about reasons to withhold belief with respect to $p$, and paradigm cases of reasons to withhold belief are *not* evidence for or against $p$.

Now I am ready to give a contrastivist view of the six types of epistemic reasons listed above. Begin with reasons to believe $p$ rather than believe $\neg p$. This is probably the easiest case: a reason to believe $p$ rather than believe $\neg p$ is simply *evidence* for $p$. Similarly, of course, a reason to believe $\neg p$ rather than believe $p$ is evidence for $\neg p$ (or evidence against $p$). Evidence for $p$ is also a reason to believe $p$ rather than withhold— the fact that Tom's fingerprints are on the book is a reason to believe that Tom stole the book, rather than withhold belief in this proposition. Of course, this reason might not be weighty enough to justify belief in this proposition, but that is compatible with saying that it is a reason to believe it. Similarly, evidence for $\neg p$ is a reason to believe $\neg p$ rather than

---

[7] For views along these lines (ignoring important differences between them), see Parfit (2001), Piller (2001, 2006), Olson (2004), Hieronymi (2005), Stratton-Lake (2005).

withhold. Let '$\text{Ev}_p$' stand for the set of evidence for $p$ and '$\text{Ev}_{\neg p}$' stand for the set of evidence for $\neg p$.

This leaves reasons to withhold rather than believe $p$ and reasons to withhold rather than believe $\neg p$. Begin with considerations like the fact that you will receive more evidence regarding $p$ tomorrow. This is both a reason to withhold rather than believe $p$ and a reason to withhold rather than believe $\neg p$. For other examples, consider the fact that you're very sleepy and won't be able to evaluate the evidence properly, the fact that you have very little evidence either way, or the fact that $p$ is completely irrelevant. Arguably, at least, these are reasons to withhold rather than believe that $p$ and reasons to withhold rather than believe that $\neg p$. They are the right kinds of considerations to make withholding belief epistemically rational. These types of reasons are both reasons to withhold rather than believe that $p$ and reasons to withhold rather than believe that $\neg p$. Call the set of such reasons for a proposition $p$ '$W_p$'.

Sometimes, though, the reasons to withhold rather than believe that $p$ and the reasons to withhold rather than believe that $\neg p$ can come apart. An advantage of contrastivism is that it gives us a very straightforward way to capture this. Stanley (2005) presents cases in which believing $p$ is very risky, while believing $\neg p$ is not, or vice versa.[8] Suppose Hannah and her wife Sarah are driving by the bank on Friday afternoon, and have paychecks to deposit. Unfortunately, the lines at the bank are very long. But Hannah remembers that she was at the bank a few weeks ago on a Saturday. In the low-stakes version of the case, we are to imagine that there's no special need for the checks to be deposited before Monday, though it would be nice to have them in before that. In this case, many people have the intuition that Hannah *knows* that the bank will be open on Saturday. In the high-stakes version, on the other hand, the checks must be deposited before Monday, or else Hannah and Sarah will lose their house. In this case, many people have the intuition that Hannah does not know that the bank will be open on Saturday. This difference in knowledge can be traced to (or perhaps results in, if you like a *knowledge-first* epistemology, as in Williamson, 2000) a difference between the two cases in the rationality of Hannah's belief that the bank will be open on

---

[8] The riskiness depends on the belief that $p$ playing its characteristic role in guiding action—to suffer the potential consequences of believing that $p$, you have actually to act as if $p$ is true.

Saturday. The belief is rational in the low-stakes case, but not in the high-stakes case. One natural explanation—though not, of course, the only explanation—of what's going on here is that the potential costs or stakes can provide reasons to withhold belief.[9]

But notice that, in the high-stakes case, there is no risk associated with *disbelieving*—with believing that the bank will *not* be open on Saturday. There seems to be an asymmetry between how stakes affect the rationality of believing and disbelieving.[10] So these stakes- or cost-provided reasons to withhold seem to be different from the reasons to withhold already mentioned, like the fact that you'll get more evidence soon. The contrastivist can explain this difference. Potential costs of believing $p$ provide reasons to withhold rather than believe $p$, but not reasons to withhold rather than disbelieve $p$. Similarly, the potential costs of falsely believing $\neg p$ provide reasons to withhold rather than believe $\neg p$, but not reasons to withhold rather than believe $p$. Let '$C_p$' stand for the set of reasons provided by potential costs of falsely believing $p$ and '$C_{\neg p}$' stand for the reasons provided by potential costs of falsely believing $\neg p$.

Finally, I claim that *evidence* can also be reason to withhold belief. Initially, this claim seems completely wrong.[11] I have already said that the fact that Tom's fingerprints are on the book is a reason to believe that Tom stole the book rather than withhold—it is a reason *not* to withhold, and to believe that Tom stole the book, instead. In general, evidence is either evidence for or against $p$, and so reasons to believe or disbelieve $p$. Both of these are rationally incompatible with withholding belief. So it is hard to see how evidence can be reason to withhold.

But remember that I am providing a contrastive account of epistemic reasons. This allows me to hold that evidence that $p$ is reason to withhold rather than believe that $\neg p$, even though it's also reason to believe that $p$ rather than withhold. Similarly, evidence that $\neg p$ is reason to withhold rather than believe that $p$. Though the fact that Tom's fingerprints are

---

[9] For more discussion of these kinds of cases, see Schroeder (2012a) which focuses on costs of believing and withholding.

[10] It may be that disbelieving is irrational, but that will be because of the evidence Hannah has that the bank will be open on Saturday (her memory that the bank was open on Saturday a few weeks ago). The stakes themselves do not seem to count against disbelieving, since the potential practical costs are associated only with believing.

[11] See Schroeder (2012a) for this kind of argument that evidence cannot be reason to withhold.

on the book is a reason to believe that Tom stole the book rather than withhold, it is also a reason to withhold belief rather than believe that Tom did not steal the book. One way to further support this claim is to notice that evidence for $p$ suggests that withholding belief would do *better* than disbelieving $p$ with respect to the epistemic goal of avoiding false beliefs. But, even if we reject this kind of instrumentalism about epistemic reasons, it seems to me plausible that evidence that $p$ is reason to withhold belief *rather than* disbelieve $p$. One way that may help you warm up to this idea is to imagine that you currently disbelieve $p$, but then get some evidence for $p$. A rational response to this may be to withhold belief; this suggests that the evidence rationalizes, and so is a reason for, withholding rather than disbelieving.

As we will see, this is the feature of this contrastive account that gives it explanatory advantages over the rival non-contrastive picture. Moreover, it seems that this kind of move is proprietary to the contrastivist—it is not clear how evidence could be reason to withhold on a non-contrastive picture. I will return to this claim later, once I have introduced the competing non-contrastive view.

So, to sum up, I have offered the following account of epistemic reasons. Let '$\oplus$' stand for the combining reasons operation:

- reasons to believe that $p$ rather than believe that $\neg p$ = reasons to believe that $p$ rather than withhold = $\mathrm{Ev}_p$
- reasons to believe that $\neg p$ rather than believe that $p$ = reasons to believe that $\neg p$ rather than withhold = $\mathrm{Ev}_{\neg p}$
- reasons to withhold rather than believe that $p$ = $W_p \oplus C_p \oplus \mathrm{Ev}_{\neg p}$
- reasons to withhold rather than believe that $\neg p$ = $W_p \oplus C_{\neg p} \oplus \mathrm{Ev}_p$

## 6.1.2 A contrastive account of rational withholding

Now we can plug this account of epistemic reasons into the principles about when an agent ought to believe a proposition, and when an agent ought to withhold belief in a proposition. Let '$A > B$' mean that the set of reasons $A$ is weightier than the set of reasons $B$.

O(Bel):  $s$ ought to believe $p$ iff (i) $\mathrm{Ev}_p > \mathrm{Ev}_{\neg p}$, and (ii) $\mathrm{Ev}_p > W_p \oplus C_p \oplus \mathrm{Ev}_{\neg p}$.

O(Wh-B):  $s$ ought to withhold belief with respect to $p$ iff (i) $W_p \oplus C_p \oplus \mathrm{Ev}_{\neg p} > \mathrm{Ev}_p$, and (ii) $W_p \oplus C_{\neg p} \oplus \mathrm{Ev}_p > \mathrm{Ev}_{\neg p}$.

This looks complicated, but, again, it is exactly what follows from the contrastive account of ought plus the account of epistemic reasons. You ought to believe that $p$ when you have most reason to believe that $p$ out of {believe $p$, believe $\neg p$}, and most reason to believe that $p$ out of {believe $p$, withhold}. You ought to withhold when you have most reason to withhold out of {believe $p$, withhold} and most reason to withhold out of {believe $\neg p$, withhold}. The complicated notation is just meant to make clear the distinctions between the different categories of reasons to withhold.

Note that condition (i) in O(Bel) is actually redundant, assuming $W_p$ and $C_p$ cannot have negative weight, and assuming that (at least in this case) the weights of the reasons to withhold combine in a broadly additive way. That is, whenever an agent has more reason to believe that $p$ than to withhold belief (out of these two options), she will also have more reason to believe that $p$ than to believe that $\neg p$ (out of these two options). This is intuitive: if your evidence for $p$ is good enough to make believing more rational than withholding, it should also be good enough to make believing more rational than disbelieving. This is a direct result, of course, of the fact that this account treats evidence that $\neg p$ as reason to withhold rather than believe that $p$, along with the assumption that there are not epistemic reasons not to withhold belief other than evidence for or against $p$. As we will see, though, the analogous condition governing when agents ought to intend will not be redundant. This is because the analog of the assumption that there are not (non-evidential) reasons against withholding belief is not plausible in the case of intention.

In the next two subsections, I will show that this contrastive account of rational withholding has explanatory advantages over an initially attractive non-contrastive account. As we will see, contrastivism has these advantages because of the claim that evidence for a proposition $p$ is not only reason to believe $p$ rather than believe $\neg p$ and reason to believe $p$ rather than withhold, but also reason to withhold rather than believe $\neg p$. As I have mentioned, and will argue further, this move is proprietary to the contrastivist.

### 6.1.3 A non-contrastive account

The picture I have developed is a contrastive implementation of a popular picture of epistemic rationality, according to which what you epistemically ought to do is determined by the strength of your epistemic reasons. In particular, according to this view, you ought to withhold belief in a proposition when your reasons for withholding are stronger than both your reasons for believing and your reasons for disbelieving. A non-contrastive version of this type of account of rational withholding is explicitly defended by Schroeder (2012a), but we can also extrapolate from claims made by other epistemologists to see that it is part of a widely accepted picture of epistemic rationality. For example, consider the following passage from Chisholm (1976: 27):

$h$ is certain for $S$ at $t =_{df}$ (i) Accepting $h$ is more reasonable for $S$ at $t$ than withholding $h$ (i.e., not accepting $h$ and not accepting $\neg h$) and (ii) there is no $i$ such that accepting $i$ is more reasonable for $S$ at $t$ than accepting $h$.

And here is a similar idea from Conee and Feldman (2004: 3):

[A] person is justified in believing a proposition when the person's evidence better supports believing it than it supports disbelieving it or suspending judgment about it.

Though these are both theses about the rationality of believing, they at least plausibly illustrate commitment to a picture according to which what you epistemically ought to do is determined by the strength of your epistemic reasons. So, if we want to generate an account of rational withholding from this picture, it would hold that you ought to withhold belief in a proposition when your epistemic reasons more strongly support withholding than they support either believing or disbelieving.

An attraction of both the contrastive theory I have presented and this non-contrastive theory is that it subsumes the account of when agents ought to withhold belief under a much more general account of when an agent ought to do *something*, where this includes performing an action and forming (or withholding) an attitude. The contrastive account is just given by CRO, as we have seen. The non-contrastive account is given by the claim that what you ought to do is what you have most reason to do. In the special case of withholding belief, then, the claim is that you ought to withhold belief when you have most reason to withhold belief—that is, more reason to withhold than for the alternatives—namely, believing and disbelieving.

Next, I will present a problem that faces this picture. The key advantage of the contrastive account of rational withholding I developed earlier in the chapter is that it avoids this problem.

### 6.1.4 Ties

When your evidence for $p$ and your evidence for $\neg p$ are balanced, or tied, you ought to withhold belief. This is a requirement on any theory of rational withholding. If we follow the popular picture of epistemic rationality introduced in the previous subsection and accept the idea that what you ought to do is what you have most reason to do, this means that, whenever your evidence is tied, you must have more reason to withhold belief than to believe $p$ or believe $\neg p$. So, when your evidence provides very little reason to believe $p$ and equally little reason to believe $\neg p$, you have to have more reason to withhold. And—crucially—when your evidence provides very strong reason to believe $p$, and equally strong reason to believe $\neg p$, you *still* have to have more reason to withhold. In general, no matter how strong your evidence for and against $p$, when it is balanced, you must have more reason to withhold belief in $p$.

What we need, then, is some explanation for why your reasons to withhold belief will always be weightier than your reasons to believe $p$ and your reasons to believe $\neg p$, no matter how weighty they are, when your evidence is tied. I'll now argue that the non-contrastive account of rational withholding cannot explain this.

The non-contrastive account can recognize two kinds of reasons to withhold belief. First, there are reasons like the fact that you will get more evidence tomorrow or that you're too sleepy properly to evaluate the evidence. Second, there are reasons provided by the stakes or potential costs of falsely believing. But note that the weights of these kinds of reasons seem to have nothing to do with whether or not your evidence is tied. So we lack an explanation for why these reasons to withhold will always outweigh both the reasons to believe $p$ and the reasons to believe $\neg p$, in cases of ties.[12]

The contrastive account I developed was able to recognize these two types of reasons to withhold belief, but also able to treat *evidence* as reason to withhold—evidence for $p$ as reason to withhold rather than disbelieve $p$ and evidence against $p$ as reason to withhold rather than believe $p$. I will explain shortly how this allows the contrastivist to explain why you ought always to withhold when your evidence for and against $p$ is tied. But it is worth pointing out here why the non-contrastive theory

---

[12] Thanks to Mark Schroeder and Selim Berker for discussion of this problem.

cannot follow the contrastivist and treat evidence as reason to withhold. If we did this, there would always be at least as much reason to withhold belief as to believe $p$ or believe $\neg p$, and ordinarily there would be most reason to withhold. That's because any reason to believe $p$—evidence for $p$—would also be reason to withhold belief, and similarly for reasons to disbelieve $p$. So neither the reasons to believe nor the reasons to disbelieve could ever outweigh the reasons to withhold, and, as long as either there were some reasons on each side or there were any additional reasons to withhold, withholding would be what there was most reason to do. Thus, if the non-contrastivist were to attempt to co-opt the strategy of treating evidence as reason to withhold, she would commit herself to the view that, in almost every case, what you ought to do is withhold belief. This would be a strange route to skepticism.

One response here is to claim that, in cases of ties, there is a special kind of reason to withhold belief:

**Meta-Reason:** The fact that your evidence is tied is a reason to withhold belief.

Thus, in cases of ties, you get a new reason to withhold belief. This is plausible.[13] But, to predict that you always ought to withhold belief in the case of ties, we need to add the following stipulation:

**Stipulation:** This Meta-Reason is always sufficiently weighty that your reasons to withhold belief outweigh both your reasons to believe that $p$ and your reasons to believe that $\neg p$.

With these two assumptions, the non-contrastive account can predict that you ought to withhold belief whenever your evidence is tied.

But I think this strategy is problematic for two reasons. First, it is simply not very explanatory. While it is plausible that the fact that your evidence is tied is a reason to withhold, it is not very explanatory simply to stipulate that it is sufficiently weighty to do the job. This comes very close simply to stipulating that, in cases of ties, you ought to withhold belief. But it would be better if we could *explain* this fact, instead.

---

[13] I say that it's plausible, but it's not obviously true. One reason to be skeptical is that the fact that your evidence is tied sounds like a *verdictive* or *overall* fact, rather than a *pro tanto* consideration. That is, it sounds like a fact that reports on the outcome of weighing up the *pro tanto* considerations, rather than itself being one of the *pro tanto* considerations.

Second, these assumptions do not go far enough. In most cases, if your evidence is *almost* tied, you still ought to withhold belief. But, if your evidence is merely *almost* tied, we cannot appeal to **Meta-Reason**, since you have this reason only when your evidence is in fact tied. We could try modifying **Meta-Reason** so that you had this sort of reason even when your evidence is merely *almost* tied. But this is starting to look very unexplanatory. Further, we need some account of *how close* to balanced your evidence for and against $p$ must be in order for this sort of meta-reason to apply. Complicating things even further, how close to balanced your evidence must be for withholding to be what you ought to do might vary with the subject matter, with the amount of available evidence, and perhaps in other ways. So we still do not have a satisfactory explanation, on the non-contrastive account, for why you always ought to withhold belief when your evidence is tied.

### 6.1.5 A contrastivist explanation

The contrastivist account I've given here, on the other hand, explains this observation nicely. To see this, assume that your evidence for $p$ and your evidence for $\neg p$ are tied; so set $Ev_p = Ev_{\neg p}$ in **O(Wh-B)** above. It is easy to see then that, in any case like this, you can never have more reason to believe $p$ than to withhold or more reason to believe $\neg p$ than to withhold. This already takes us much closer to explaining why you always ought to withhold belief in such cases. And, as long as there is always either (i) *some* cost of falsely believing, so that, $C_p$ and $C_{\neg p}$ are not completely empty, or (ii) some reason to withhold rather than either believe $p$ or believe $\neg p$, so that, $W_p$ is not empty, it will turn out that in every case in which your evidence is tied, you ought to withhold out of {believe $p$, believe $\neg p$, withhold}.

It is very plausible that at least one of (i) and (ii) is true. I acknowledge, though, that for my account to make the prediction that you ought to withhold in cases of ties, I do need one of (i) and (ii) to be true. One way we could guarantee this is to accept a contrastivist version of **Meta-Reason**: the fact that your evidence is tied is always a reason to withhold rather than believe $p$ and a reason to withhold rather than believe $\neg p$. Then $W_p$ will not be completely empty in cases of ties.

Notice that this strategy does not require accepting the unexplanatory **Stipulation** that this meta-reason is always sufficiently weighty. Rather, it would *explain* why it was sufficiently weighty: in cases of ties, all you need, according to O(Wh-B), is *some* reason in $W_p$, so the meta-reason will always be weighty enough. If there are cases of ties in which neither (i) nor (ii) is true, my account can at least explain why it is never the case that you have more reason to believe than to withhold, or more reason to disbelieve than to withhold—that is, you will always have at least as much reason to withhold as to believe or to disbelieve. The non-contrastive account cannot explain this.

Moreover, the contrastive account can explain why you ought to withhold belief, even in many cases in which your evidence is not quite tied. As long as there are either (i) potential costs of falsely believing or (ii) reasons to withhold rather than either believe $p$ or believe $\neg p$ that are sufficiently weighty to outweigh the difference in the strength of the evidence for $p$ and for $\neg p$, you ought to withhold. So this account tells us how close to balanced your evidence must be in order for withholding to be what you ought to do. The difference must be small enough for the potential costs of falsely believing and your reasons to withhold in $W_p$ to outweigh it. This explains why we get the sort of variation I mentioned: in cases in which you have very weighty reasons to withhold, in $W_p$, or in which the stakes are very high (as in Stanley's bank cases (2005)), you ought to withhold belief even if your evidence is quite unbalanced. In lower-stakes cases in which you don't have very weighty reasons to withhold in $W_p$, your evidence must be much closer to balanced for withholding to be what you ought to do.

For this explanation to work, it is also important that we adopt the principle **CRO** relating an agent's contrastive reasons to what she ought to do. Recall that this principle says that to determine what an agent ought to do out of a set $Q$, we look not at the reasons relative to the entire set $Q$, but instead at the pairwise subsets:

**CRO:** $s$ ought to $A$ out of $Q$ iff $s$ has most reason to $A$ out of $\{A, B\}$, for all of the other alternatives $B$ in $Q$.

In Chapter 3, I argued that this Condorcet-like principle is preferable to the following principle:

**CRO\*:** $s$ ought to $A$ out of $Q$ iff $s$ has most reason to $A$ out of $Q$.

The problem with **CRO\*** is that it does not deliver the correct results in cases in which the best alternative is not best along any one dimension, but best on balance. **CRO** does better in these cases. Now we can see another advantage of CRO over CRO*. If we accepted CRO*, and held that both evidence for $p$ and evidence against $p$ also provide reasons to withhold, we would get the result that you nearly always ought to withhold belief, just as we would if we treated evidence as reason to withhold on the non-contrastive view, as we have seen. The evidence for $p$ would give you some reason to believe $p$, but also reason to withhold; similarly for evidence against $p$. So you will always have at least as much reason to withhold as to believe or disbelieve, and, as long as there is some evidence on each side, or some other non-evidential reason to withhold, withholding would be what you ought to do.[14] So, if we accepted CRO* instead of CRO, the contrastivist would have no advantage over the non-contrastivist. In fact, if {believe, disbelieve, withhold} is an *exhaustive* set, then accepting CRO* would collapse our account in the non-contrastive view, at least in this respect.

### 6.1.6 Reasons not to withhold belief?

I have been assuming that there are no epistemic reasons not to withhold belief, other than evidence. This is an important assumption, since, if we allow for such reasons, the principle that you ought to withhold belief whenever your evidence is tied may be false. It may be that, even if your evidence is tied, you have sufficiently strong reason not to withhold belief, so that you ought not to withhold. My argument against the non-contrastive view was based on this principle.

I know of two kinds of potential counterexamples to the principle, both of which involve apparent reasons not to withhold belief. The first, suggested by Mark van Roojen, is the following.[15] You are on an interview committee, getting ready to interview shortlisted candidates. You've read their applications, and think that the information there does not settle the question of who is the best candidate—you'll need to gather more information in the in-person interview. However, you also know that frequently we humans tend to significantly over- or underweight certain kinds of information that we gather from in-person interviews, owing to

---

[14] This would actually require rejecting the analysis of what it takes for some consideration to be a reason for an alternative that I defended in Chapter 4, since that analysis would predict that the evidence could be reason for at most one of believing and withholding. But otherwise we can't even make sense of the claim that evidence is reason for both believing and withholding, out of {believe, disbelieve, withhold}.

[15] This case is from a comment on the PEA Soup blog: http://peasoup.typepad.com/peasoup/2012/06/i.html (accessed 7 October 2016).

implicit biases. You also know that, if you make up your mind, at least tentatively, beforehand, these distorting factors are much less significant. If you go into the in-person interviews with a view about who the best candidate is, you will weight the evidence appropriately, and come to a better judgment, even if this involves revising your initial view. In such a case, van Roojen suggests, these considerations about bias and how to avoid it may provide reason not to withhold belief.

The second case is from Turri (2012). You are waiting outside a meeting of the world's best mathematicians, who are meeting to try to prove or disprove an important conjecture. As the mathematicians come out, looking pleased with themselves, you ask about the results. One of them smiles and tells you, "Well, I'll tell you this: you should not withhold belief." Turri thinks this gives you a testimonial reason not to withhold belief; after all, if the mathematician had advised you to withhold belief, that would pretty clearly be a reason to withhold belief.

In response to Turri's case, I think that Comesaña (2013) is correct that in fact the mathematician's testimony gives you reason to withhold belief, rather than reason not to withhold belief. In response to van Roojen's case, my inclination is to think of it as one in which you have good reason to *accept* some hypothesis about who the best candidate is, rather than settle on a belief. But I recognize that the case may be spelled out so that you won't get the bias-reducing benefits unless you actually form a belief.

So my fallback reply is to point out that, even if these are cases in which we have reasons not to withhold belief, it is still true that in many cases in which your evidence is tied, or nearly tied, you ought to withhold belief. Some of these cases are ones in which you have very strong evidential reason to believe and (nearly) equally strong reason to disbelieve. The non-contrastive view will have no explanation of this, since we still have no reason to expect the reasons to withhold recognized by that view to outweigh the evidential reasons. So my argument did not, strictly speaking, require the truth of the principle about ties.

## 6.2 Withholding Intention

Just as agents often ought to withhold belief in a given proposition, they often ought to withhold intention, with respect to a given action. For example, suppose I've been invited to a party next weekend. I'd like to go, but there's a chance an old friend will be in town the evening of the party, and, if she is, then I should see her. I will know in the next couple of days if she will in fact make the trip. In this case, the thing for me to do is withhold intention about whether to go to the party. I shouldn't intend to go, since my friend may be in town, and I shouldn't intend *not* to go to the party, since she may not be. Rather, I should withhold intention until I get more information. Now that I have provided the contrastivist account of when agents ought to withhold belief, I want to generalize to an account of when agents ought to withhold attitudes that apply not only to belief but also to intention.

### 6.2.1 A unified account?

My goal is to give a unified account of rational withholding that applies to both the practical and theoretical cases. Besides the theoretical virtues, there are also striking structural similarities between withholding intention and withholding belief that make it reasonable to expect such a unified account. In both cases, there is what we might call the 'positive' attitude—believing $p$ or intending to $\phi$; the 'negative' attitude—believing $\neg p$ or intending not to $\phi$; and the 'undecided' attitude—withholding belief or withholding intention.[16]

But Harman (2004) makes an observation that seems to raise a problem for this idea. He points out that there is, at least in many cases, an important difference between the theoretical and practical cases with respect to what you ought to do when your reasons for the positive and negative attitude are tied. In the practical case, it is generally permissible simply to decide. In fact, it's often *im*permissible *not* to decide, even if your reasons to intend to $\phi$ and reasons to intend not to $\phi$ are tied. Think of the case of Buridan's Ass, who starved to death trying to decide whether to take the bale of hay on the right or the identical bale on the left. Since the reasons to intend to take the bale on the right were perfectly matched by reasons to intend to take the bale on the left, it withheld intention about whether to take the bale of hay on the right (as well as about whether to take the bale of hay on the left), and ended up starving to death. But things are different in the theoretical case. When your reasons to believe

---

[16] By calling believing $\neg p$ and intending not to $\phi$ 'negative', I don't mean to suggest that there are any deep differences between these and what I called the 'positive' attitudes. This is especially obvious in the case of belief: believing that $\neg p$ is simply bearing the same attitude—believing—to a different proposition. Perhaps there's some more important difference between intending to $\psi$, where $\psi$ is incompatible with $\phi$, and intending not to $\phi$. But I'll ignore this issue here.

*p* and your reasons to believe ¬*p* are tied, it is in general *not* rationally permissible just to pick one to believe. In this case, you ought to withhold belief. Since cases of ties are cases in which you ought to withhold belief but not, or not always, cases in which you ought to withhold intention, it looks like we can't give a unified account of when you ought to withhold that applies to both.

Harman's observation is correct—it is often (practically) permissible simply to form an intention to $\phi$ or an intention not to $\phi$ when your reasons for each are tied, and it is never (epistemically) permissible simply to form a belief in *p* or a belief in ¬*p* when your reasons for each are tied. But it is a mistake to conclude that this must be due to any structural differences between the correct accounts of when you ought to withhold intention, on one hand, and belief, on the other. Rather, we can explain the asymmetry Harman observes by noticing that, though there are frequently weighty reasons *not* to withhold intention (for example, you'll starve to death, if you do), there are never, or at least very rarely, reasons not to withhold belief (besides, of course, evidence). Thus, we should actually expect the asymmetry Harman observes, even if we have a unified account of rational withholding. It is just that, in the practical case, it will often be hard for the reasons to withhold intention to outweigh the reasons not to withhold intention, but this will not be true for withholding belief.[17]

### 6.2.2 Contrastive practical reasons

Now I will provide an account of what I'll call, for the purposes of this chapter, *practical* reasons. By this I simply mean reasons that bear on what practical attitude—intending to $\phi$, intending not to $\phi$, or withholding intention—it is rational for you to take toward a given action, $\phi$. This is to use the term 'practical reasons' in a different way from how it is often used. This term is often used to refer to reasons for *action* rather than reasons for intention. But again, since I am talking about intentions, I am just talking about reasons for forming or withholding intentions.

Just as I restricted my discussion in the epistemic case to epistemic reasons, ignoring reasons like the fact that a demon has threatened to kill you if you believe that *p*, I will here restrict my discussion to practical reasons that bear on whether it is rational to intend to $\phi$, intend not to

---

[17] Schroeder (2012a) brings out essentially the same point, but in a different way.

$\phi$, or withhold intention. So I will set aside reasons like those present in Kavka's Toxin Puzzle (1983). In this case, you are offered a lot of money to intend to drink a mild toxin, with the catch that you know you will receive the money before the time comes to drink the toxin. In this case, you have a reason to intend to drink the toxin that is importantly different from a reason like the fact that someone else will give you a lot of money if you actually drink the toxin, or the fact that the toxin is tasty. I do not have a good way to distinguish between these right kind and wrong kind of reasons in the practical case, just as I had no good way to distinguish between the right kind and wrong kind of reasons in the epistemic case. But, rather than entering into this important but difficult debate, I will rely on an intuitive understanding of the difference, and only talk about reasons that, I hope, fall clearly on the right kind side.

I am concerned here with the question of what attitude an agent ought to take toward an action, $\phi$. So the relevant alternatives will be intending to $\phi$, intending not to $\phi$, or withholding intention. As before, we can simply appeal to CRO. Applying CRO to the case of intention, we get the following principles:

> **O(Int)\*:** $s$ ought to intend to $\phi$ iff (i) $s$ has most reason to intend to $\phi$ out of {intend to $\phi$, intend not to $\phi$} and (ii) $s$ has most reason to intend to $\phi$ out of {intend to $\phi$, withhold intention}.
>
> **O(Wh-I)\*:** $s$ ought to withhold intention with respect to $\phi$ iff (i) $s$ has most reason to withhold intention out of {intend to $\phi$, withhold intention} and (ii) $s$ has most reason to withhold intention out of {intend not to $\phi$, withhold intention}.

So what we need is some account of what these reasons are: (i) reasons to intend to $\phi$ rather than intend not to $\phi$, (ii) reasons to intend to $\phi$ rather than withhold, (iii) reasons to intend not to $\phi$ rather than intend to $\phi$, (iv) reasons to intend not to $\phi$ rather than withhold, (v) reasons to withhold rather than intend to $\phi$, and (vi) reasons to withhold rather than intend not to $\phi$.

Perhaps the easiest cases are reasons to intend to $\phi$ rather than intend not to $\phi$, and reasons to intend not to $\phi$ rather than intend to $\phi$. These are simply reasons for and against $\phi$-ing, respectively. Similarly, reasons for and against $\phi$-ing will be among the reasons to intend to $\phi$ rather than withhold, and to intend not to $\phi$, rather than withhold, respectively. Call these sets of reasons '$R_\phi$' and '$R_{ag-\phi}$'.

As a contrastivist, though, I need to say what sets these reasons for and against $\phi$-ing are relativized to. I conceive of things as follows. Deliberating agents face two subtly different kinds of questions. First, there is the kind of question I have been dealing with in most of the book, the question of what to do. This question will ordinarily provide a set of alternative actions, like $\{\phi, \psi, \chi\}$. Second, the agent will face the kind of question I have been considering in this chapter, the question of whether to (intend to) $\phi$. This question will provide a set of alternatives like the one I am concerned with here, {intend to $\phi$, intend not to $\phi$, withhold intention}. So the reasons for and against $\phi$-ing will be relativized to the contextually relevant set, like $\{\phi, \psi, \chi\}$. The reasons to $\phi$ relative to this set will then also be reasons to intend to $\phi$ rather than intend not to $\phi$, and to intend to $\phi$ rather than withhold intention. The reasons not to $\phi$, $R_{ag\text{-}\phi}$, will also be reasons to intend not to $\phi$ rather than intend to $\phi$, and to intend not to $\phi$ rather than withhold intention.

But, in addition, we need to account for some other reasons not to withhold—or, on this framework, reasons to intend to $\phi$ rather than withhold and to intend not to $\phi$ rather than withhold. These will include considerations like the fact that you will starve to death if you withhold intention. For a more realistic example of reasons not to withhold intention, notice that agents often simply have to decide because the time to act has come. If you are trying to decide whether to go see the guest speaker today, at some point—say, shortly before the talk is scheduled to start—you simply have to make up your mind. Another related source of reasons not to withhold intention comes from the fact that intentions aid in coordination, as emphasized by Bratman (1987). Forming intentions can aid in your own planning and in making joint plans with others. You miss out on these benefits if you withhold intention.[18] Thus, these considerations about coordination can provide reasons to intend to $\phi$ rather than withhold, and reasons to intend not to $\phi$ rather than withhold. Notice how common these kinds of reasons are. This reinforces the point above that there are frequently reasons not to withhold intention, and this lets us explain Harman's observation. Call the set of such reasons '$\neg W_\phi$'.

That just leaves reasons to withhold rather than intend to $\phi$ and reasons to withhold rather than intend not to $\phi$. In the epistemic case, we had reasons in the set $W_p$, like the fact that you'll get more information regarding

---

[18] To be more careful: you get these benefits only if you form an intention.

$p$ tomorrow, or the fact that you simply don't have very much evidence one way or the other. These are reasons to withhold belief rather than believe $p$ and to withhold belief rather than believe $\neg p$. Analogously, in the case of intention, there are reasons to withhold intention rather than intend to $\phi$ and to withhold intention rather than intend not to $\phi$. For example, the fact that you'll get more relevant information tomorrow is such a reason. For another example, the fact that there's no pressing need to make up your mind yet (for example, there's no one to coordinate with, not much advance planning required, and the time to $\phi$, if you do it at all, isn't for several months) is also a reason to withhold intention rather than either intend to $\phi$ or intend not to $\phi$. Call the set of reasons like this '$W_\phi$'.

Just as the reasons to withhold belief rather than believe $p$ could come apart from the reasons to withhold belief rather than believe $\neg p$, the reasons to withhold intention rather than intend to $\phi$ may come apart from the reasons to withhold intention rather than intend not to $\phi$. First, there may be particular costs associated with intending to $\phi$ that are not associated with intending not to $\phi$, or vice versa. Suppose that intending to $\phi$ cuts off some other options that are desirable in certain ways, while intending not to $\phi$ does not. This is plausible, given the coordinating role of intention, especially in the interpersonal case. Forming intentions to do or not to do certain things will lead others to form intentions that may then disqualify certain options that would otherwise be open to you. These kinds of costs can provide reasons to withhold rather than intend to $\phi$ that are not reasons to withhold rather than intend not to $\phi$ (or vice versa). Call the set of such reasons '$C_\phi$' and '$C_{not\text{-}\phi}$', respectively.

Finally, just as I held that evidence for $p$ provides reasons to withhold rather than believe that $\neg p$, I hold that reasons to $\phi$, $R_\phi$, are also reasons to withhold intention rather than intend not to $\phi$, and that reasons not to $\phi$, $R_{ag\text{-}\phi}$, are also reasons to withhold rather than intend to $\phi$.

### 6.2.3 A contrastive account of rational withholding of intention

Now we can plug these reasons into the principles O(Int)* and O(Wh-I)* to get the account of when agents ought to intend and when they ought to withhold intention:

O(Int): $s$ ought to intend to $\phi$ iff (i) $R_\phi > R_{ag\text{-}\phi}$, and (ii) $R_\phi \oplus \neg W_\phi > R_{ag\text{-}\phi} \oplus C_\phi \oplus W_\phi$.

**O(Wh-I)**: $s$ ought to withhold intention with respect to $\phi$ iff (i) $W_\phi \oplus C_\phi \oplus R_{ag\text{-}\phi} > R_\phi \oplus \neg W_\phi$, and (ii) $W_\phi \oplus C_{not\text{-}\phi} \oplus R_\phi > R_{ag\text{-}\phi} \oplus \neg W_\phi$.

As I said above, condition (i) in **O(Int)** is not redundant, as the analogous clause was in the epistemic case, **O(Bel)**. In the epistemic case, as long as an agent has more reason to believe that $p$ than to withhold (out of those two options), she was guaranteed to have more reason to believe that $p$ than to believe that $\neg p$ (out of those two options). This relied on the assumption that there are not epistemic reasons not to withhold belief. But, as I said in defending the possibility of a unified account of rational withholding, there frequently are reasons not to withhold intention. On the contrastivist view I'm developing here, these are the reasons to intend to $\phi$ rather than withhold and reasons to intend not to $\phi$ rather than withhold—$\neg W_\phi$. The upshot here is that an agent may have more reason to intend to $\phi$ than to withhold intention (out of those two options) without having more reason to intend to $\phi$ rather than to intend not to $\phi$. In fact, this kind of thing seems to happen frequently. I have to settle on an intention to go to the talk or an intention not to go to the talk—I can't just keep deliberating forever—even if neither of these options is more attractive than the other.

In the epistemic case, I claimed that, whenever your evidence for and against $p$ is tied, you ought to withhold belief. The analogous claim is not true in the practical case, as Harman observed. Sometimes you just have to decide. But it is still true that, in *some* cases in which your reasons for and against $\phi$-ing are tied, you ought to withhold intention. And, crucially, there are both cases in which you ought to withhold and have very little reason either way, and cases in which you ought to withhold and have strong reasons each way. So we still need an explanation for why your reasons to withhold intention are weightier than your reasons to intend to $\phi$ and your reasons to intend not to $\phi$ in these cases.

A non-contrastivist account analogous to the non-contrastive epistemic account discussed in Section 6.1.3 will not have such an explanation. That is because the weights of the kinds of reasons to withhold that this kind of account could recognize—the fact that you'll get more information before the time for action, costs of closing deliberation, and so on—seem to have nothing to do with the weight of your reasons to $\phi$ and the weight of your reasons not to $\phi$.

But the account I've developed here, captured in O(Wh-I), can provide such an explanation of how your reasons to withhold intention could vary in the necessary ways with the weights of your reasons to $\phi$ and your reasons not to $\phi$. And, just as in the epistemic case, this feature comes from the move, proprietary to the contrastivist, that reasons to $\phi$ are also reasons to withhold intention rather than intend not to $\phi$, and reasons not to $\phi$ are also reasons to withhold intention rather than intend to $\phi$.

Finally, just as in the epistemic case, this account can explain why sometimes you ought to withhold intention even if your reasons to $\phi$ and reasons not to $\phi$ are merely *almost* tied. As long as they are close enough to be outweighed by (i) the reasons to withhold intention in $W_\phi$ and (ii) the costs of settling deliberation, and there aren't weighty reasons not to withhold intention, you ought to withhold intention.

### 6.2.4 A unified account

So far I have shown how the following two principles make attractive predictions about when an agent ought to withhold belief and intention, respectively:

O(Wh-B): $s$ ought to withhold belief with respect to $p$ iff (i) $W_p \oplus C_p \oplus \text{Ev}_{\neg p} > \text{Ev}_p$, and (ii) $W_p \oplus C_{\neg p} \oplus \text{Ev}_p > \text{Ev}_{\neg p}$.

O(Wh-I): $s$ ought to withhold intention with respect to $\phi$ iff (i) $W_\phi \oplus C_\phi \oplus R_{ag\text{-}\phi} > R_\phi \oplus \neg W_\phi$, and (ii) $W_\phi \oplus C_{not\text{-}\phi} \oplus R_\phi > R_{ag\text{-}\phi} \oplus \neg W_\phi$.

These two principles are structurally identical, other than the addition of '$\neg W_\phi$'—reasons not to withhold intention—in O(Wh-I). Given the (somewhat controversial) assumption that there are not reasons not to withhold belief, we can simply add to O(Wh-B) an empty set, '$\neg W_p$,' without changing anything substantive about the account. Then the two principles are structurally identical, giving us a unified account of when agents ought to withhold that applies to both belief and intention, where $\pi$ is a variable ranging over contents of attitudes—either propositions or actions.

O(Wh): $s$ ought to withhold attitude $\alpha$ with respect to content $\pi$ iff (i) $W_\pi \oplus C_\pi \oplus R_{\neg\pi} > R_\pi \oplus \neg W_\pi$, and (ii) $W_\pi \oplus C_{\neg\pi} \oplus R_\pi > R_{\neg\pi} \oplus \neg W_\pi$.

Moreover, this account is just a special case of the much more general principle relating an agent's reasons with what she ought to do, CRO. Thus, the contrastivist view I have developed in this book provides an attractive account of when agents ought to withhold that can solve problems facing otherwise attractive non-contrastive views. Crucially, as I've argued, the advantages of the contrastive account actually come from contrastivism: only the contrastivist, it seems, can allow (i) evidence to be reasons to withhold belief, rather than the appropriate alternative, and (ii) reasons for action to be reasons to withhold intention, rather than the appropriate alternative.

## 6.3 Wrap Up

In this chapter I've argued that the contrastivist can give an attractive account of when one ought to withhold both belief and intention. Given the importance of withholding and the problems facing other accounts, if I'm right, then this is a compelling argument in favor of contrastivism about reasons. Moreover, this chapter and the previous one show that contrastivism has interesting applications in areas in which reasons are important, including ethics, practical reasoning, and epistemology.

I've argued in this book for contrastivism about reasons. After introducing the project in Chapter 1, I began, in Chapter 2, by arguing that our talk about reasons supports a contrastive semantics for 'reason'. I then argued, in Chapter 3, that we shouldn't stop there: normative favoring itself is contrastive. And finally, in Chapter 4, I developed the theory in more detail by analyzing reasons in terms of promotion—a popular strategy that itself provides independent support for contrastivism. Moreover, the theory I developed in Chapter 4 provides some needed constraints on the independence of reasons relative to different sets of alternatives, giving the theory structure. In Chapters 5 and 6, I provided some applications of the theory I developed in Chapters 2 through 4. I think that, taken together, all of this gives us strong reason to accept contrastivism, rather than either reject it or withhold. There is clearly much more work to be done, but I hope to have shown that theorizing about reasons within a contrastive framework is likely to be fruitful.

# References

Alvarez, Maria (2010). *Kinds of Reasons*. Oxford: Oxford University Press.
Anderson, Elizabeth (1993). *Value in Ethics and Economics*. Cambridge, MA: Harvard University Press.
Baron, Marcia, Pettit, Philip, and Slote, Michael (1997). *Three Methods of Ethics: A Debate*. Oxford: Blackwell Publishers.
Bedke, Matthew (2012). 'Ends to Means: Transmitted Reasons and their Weights'. Unpublished manuscript, University of British Columbia.
Behrends, Jeff, and DiPaolo, Joshua (2011). 'Finlay and Schroeder on Promoting a Desire'. *Journal of Ethics and Social Philosophy* (December), 1–7.
Blaauw, Martijn (2012). 'Contrastive Belief', in M. Blaauw (ed.), *Contrastivism in Philosophy*. London: Routledge, 88–100.
Bratman, Michael (1987). *Intention, Plans, and Practical Reason*. Cambridge, MA: Harvard University Press.
Broome, John (1991). *Weighing Goods*. Oxford: Blackwell Publishers.
Broome, John (1999). 'Incommensurable Value', in Roger Crisp and Brad Hooker (eds), *Well-Being and Morality: Essays in Honour of James Griffin*. Oxford: Oxford University Press, 21–38.
Broome, John (2004). 'Reasons', in R. Jay Wallace, Philip Pettit, Samuel Scheffler, and Michael Smith (eds), *Reason and Value: Themes from the Moral Philosophy of Joseph Raz*. Oxford: Oxford University Press, 28–55.
Broome, John (2013). *Rationality through Reasoning*. Oxford: Wiley-Blackwell.
Cariani, Fabrizio (2009). 'The Semantics of "Ought" and the Unity of Modal Discourse', Ph.D. thesis, University of California, Berkeley.
Cariani, Fabrizio (2013). ' "Ought" and Resolution Semantics', *Noûs*, 47/3: 534–58.
Chandler, Jake (2007). 'Solving the Tacking Problem with Contrast Classes', *British Journal for the Philosophy of Science*, 58/3: 489–502.
Chandler, Jake (2013). 'Contrastive Confirmation: Some Competing Accounts', *Synthese*, 190/1: 129–38.
Chisholm, Roderick (1976). *Person and Object*. La Salle, IL: Open Court.
Coates, D. Justin (2014). 'An Actual-Sequence Theory of Promotion', *Journal of Ethics and Social Philosophy* (January), 1–7.
Comesaña, Juan (2013). 'On a Puzzle about Withholding', *Philosophical Quarterly*, 63/251: 374–6.
Conee, Earl, and Feldman, Richard (2004). *Evidentialism: Essays in Epistemology*. Oxford: Oxford University Press.

Crisp, Roger (2000). 'Particularizing Particularism', in Brad Hooker and Margaret Little (eds), *Moral Particularism*. Oxford: Oxford University Press, 23–47.
Dancy, Jonathan (1993). *Moral Reasons*. Oxford: Blackwell Publishers.
Dancy, Jonathan (2000). *Practical Reality*. Oxford: Oxford University Press.
Dancy, Jonathan (2004). *Ethics without Principles*. Oxford: Oxford University Press.
Danielsson, Sven, and Olson, Jonas (2007). 'Brentano and the Buck-Passers', *Mind*, 116: 511–22.
D'Arms, Justin, and Jacobson, Daniel (2000a). 'The Moralistic Fallacy: On the "Appropriateness" of Emotions', *Philosophy and Phenomenological Research*, 61/1: 65–90.
D'Arms, Justin, and Jacobson, Daniel (2000b). 'Sentiment and Value', *Ethics*, 110/4: 722–48.
Darwall, Stephen (1983). *Impartial Reason*. Ithaca, NY: Cornell University Press.
Dretske, Fred (1970). 'Epistemic Operators', *Journal of Philosophy*, 67: 1007–23.
Evers, Daan (2009). 'Humean Agent-Neutral Reasons?', *Philosophical Explorations*, 12/1: 55–67.
Finlay, Stephen (2001). 'What Does Value Matter? The Interest-Relational Theory of the Semantics and Metaphysics of Value', Ph.D. thesis, University of Illinois, Urbana-Champaign.
Finlay, Stephen (2006). 'The Reasons that Matter', *Australasian Journal of Philosophy*, 84/1: 1–20.
Finlay, Stephen (2009). 'Oughts and Ends', *Philosophical Studies*, 143: 315–40.
Finlay, Stephen (2014). *Confusion of Tongues*. Oxford: Oxford University Press.
Finlay, Stephen, and Snedegar, Justin (2014). 'One "Ought" too Many', *Philosophy and Phenomenological Research*, 89/1: 102–24.
Fitelson, Branden (2012). 'Contrastive Bayesianism', in Martijn Blaauw (ed.), *Contrastivism in Philosophy*. London: Routledge, 64–87.
van Fraassen, Bas (1980). *The Scientific Image*. Oxford: Oxford University Press.
Friedman, Alex (2009). 'Intransitive Ethics', *Journal of Moral Philosophy*, 6: 277–97.
Friedman, Jane (2013a). 'Rational Agnosticism and Degrees of Belief', in Tamar Szabó Gendler and John Hawthorne (eds), *Oxford Studies in Epistemology*, iv. Oxford: Oxford University Press, 57–81.
Friedman, Jane (2013b). 'Suspended Judgment', *Philosophical Studies*, 162/2: 165–81.
Garfinkel, Alan (1981). *Forms of Explanation: Rethinking the Questions in Social Theory*. New Haven, CT: Yale University Press.
Greenspan, Patricia (2005). 'Asymmetrical Practical Reasons', in M. Reicher and J. Marek (eds), *Experience and Analysis: Proceedings of the 27th International Wittgenstein Symposium*. Vienna: Öbv & Hpt, 387–94.

Greenspan, P. (2007). 'Practical Reasons and Moral "Ought"', in R. Shafer-Landau (ed.), *Oxford Studies in Metaethics*, ii. Oxford: Oxford University Press, 172–94.

Grice, H. P. (1989). 'Logic and Conversation', in H. P. Grice, *Studies in the Way of Words*. Cambridge, MA: Harvard University Press, 22–40.

Groenendijk, Jeroen, and Stokhof, Martin (1997). 'Questions', in J. van Benthem and A. ter Meulen (eds), *Handbook of Logic and Language*. London: Elsevier Science Publishers, 1055–124.

Hamblin, C. L. (1958). 'Questions', *Australasian Journal of Philosophy*, 36: 159–68.

Hampton, Jean (1998). *The Authority of Reason*. Cambridge: Cambridge University Press.

Harman, Gilbert (2004). 'Practical Aspects of Theoretical Reasoning', in A. Mele and P. Rawling (eds), *The Oxford Handbook of Rationality*. Oxford: Oxford University Press, 45–56.

Hieronymi, Pamela (2005). 'The Wrong Kind of Reason', *Journal of Philosophy*, 102/9: 437–57.

Higginbotham, James (1993). 'Interrogatives', in K. Hale and S. J. Keyser (eds), *The View from Building 20: Essays in Honor of Sylvain Bromberger*. Cambridge, MA: MIT Press, 195–228.

Higginbotham, James (1996). 'The Semantics of Questions', in S. Lappin (ed.), *The Handbook of Contemporary Semantic Theory*. Oxford: Oxford University Press, 361–83.

Hitchcock, Christopher (1996). 'The Role of Contrast in Causal and Explanatory Claims', *Synthese*, 107/3: 395–419.

Horty, John (2007). 'Reasons as Defaults', *Philosophers' Imprint*, 7/3: 1–28.

Horty, John (2012). *Reasons as Defaults*. Oxford: Oxford University Press.

Jackson, Frank (1985). 'On the Semantics and Logic of Obligation', *Mind*, 94/374: 177–95.

Jackson, Frank, and Pargetter, Robert (1986). 'Oughts, Options, and Actualism', *Philosophical Review*, 95/2: 233–55.

Kavka, Gregory (1983). 'The Toxin Puzzle', *Analysis*, 43/1: 33–6.

Kierland, Brian (2012). 'A New Approach to the Future Dependence Issue', unpublished manuscript, Boise State University.

Kolodny, Niko (forthcoming). 'Instrumental Reasons', in D. Star (ed.), *Oxford Handbook of Reasons and Normativity*. Oxford: Oxford University Press.

Kratzer, Angelika (1981). 'The Notional Category of Modality', in H. J. Eikmeyer and H. Rieser (eds), *Words, Worlds, and Contexts*. Berlin: de Gruyter, 38–74.

Lehrer, Keith, and Paxson, Thomas (1969). 'Knowledge: Undefeated Justified True Belief', *Journal of Philosophy*, 66/4: 225–37.

Lewis, David (1996). 'Elusive Knowledge', *Australasian Journal of Philosophy*, 74: 549–67.

Lin, Eden (2016). 'Simple Probabilistic Promotion', *Philosophy and Phenomenological Research*, Early View.

Lipton, Peter (1990). 'Contrastive Explanation', *Royal Institute for Philosophy Supplement*, 27: 247–66.

Moore, G. E. (1903). *Principia Ethica*. Cambridge: Cambridge University Press.

Moore, G. E. (1912). *Ethics*. London: Williams & Norgate.

Morton, Adam, and Karjalainen, Antii (2003). 'Contrastive Knowledge', *Philosophical Explorations*, 6/2: 74–89.

Nagel, Thomas (1970). *The Possibility of Altruism*. Princeton, NJ: Princeton University Press.

Norcross, Alastair (1997). 'Good and Bad Actions', *Philosophical Review*, 106/1: 1–34.

Norcross, Alastair (2005a). 'Contextualism for Consequentialists', *Acta Analytica*, 20/2: 80–90.

Norcross, Alastair (2005b). 'Harming in Context', *Philosophical Studies*, 123/1–2: 149–73.

Olson, Jonas (2004). 'Buck-Passing and the Wrong-Kind of Reasons', *Philosophical Quarterly*, 54/3: 295–300.

Parfit, Derek (1984). *Reasons and Persons*. Oxford: Oxford University Press.

Parfit, D. (2001). 'Rationality and Reasons', in Dan Egonsson, Jonas Josefsson, Bjorn Petterson, and Toni Rønnow-Rasmussen (eds), *Exploring Practical Philosophy: From Action to Values*. Burlington, VT: Ashgate, 17–39.

Parfit, D. (2011). *On What Matters*. Oxford: Oxford University Press.

Pettit, Philip (1991). 'Consequentialism', in P. Singer (ed.), *A Companion to Ethics*. Oxford: Blackwell Publishers, 230–7.

Piller, Christian (2001). 'Normative Practical Reasoning', *Proceedings of the Aristotelian Society*, 25: 195–216.

Piller, Christian (2006). 'Content-Related and Attitude-Related Reasons for Preferences', *Philosophy*, 59: 155–81.

Rabinowicz, Wlodek, and Rønnow-Rasmussen, Toni (2004). 'The Strike of the Demon: On Fitting Pro-Attitudes and Value', *Ethics*, 114/3: 391–423.

Rachels, Stuart (1998). 'Counterexamples to the Transitivity of "Better than"', *Australasian Journal of Philosophy*, 76/1: 71–83.

Rachels, Stuart (2001). 'A Set of Solutions to Parfit's Problems', *Noûs*, 35: 214–38.

Raz, J. (1999). *Engaging Reason: On the Theory of Value and Action*. Oxford: Oxford University Press.

Reisner, Andrew (2009). 'Abandoning the Buck-Passing Analysis of Final Value', *Ethical Theory and Moral Practice*, 12/4: 379–95.

Rickless, Samuel (2014). 'The Contrast-Insensitivity of Knowledge Ascriptions', *Philosophy and Phenomenological Research*, 88: 533–55.

Roberts, Craige (2012). 'Information Structure in Discourse: Towards an Integrated Formal Theory of Pragmatics', *Semantics and Pragmatics*, 5: 1–69.

Rooth, Mats (1992). 'A Theory of Focus Interpretation', *Natural Language Semantics*, 1: 75–116.

Ross, Jacob (2006). 'Acceptance and Practical Reason'. Ph.D. thesis, Rutgers University.

Ruben, David-Hillel (1987). 'Explaining Contrastive Facts', *Analysis*, 47/1: 35–7.

Ruben, David-Hillel (2009). 'Con-Reasons as Causes', in C. Sandis (ed.), *New Essays on the Explanation of Action*. Basingstoke: Palgrave Macmillan, 62–74.

Scanlon, T. M. (1998). *What We Owe to Each Other*. Cambridge, MA: Harvard University Press.

Scanlon, T. (2014). *Being Realistic about Reasons*. Oxford: Oxford University Press.

Schaffer, Jonathan (2004). 'From Contextualism to Contrastivism', *Philosophical Studies*, 119/1–2: 73–104.

Schaffer, Jonathan (2005a). 'Contrastive Causation', *Philosophical Review*, 114/3: 327–58.

Schaffer, Jonathan (2005b). 'Contrastive Knowledge', in Tamar Szabó Gendler and John Hawthorne (eds), *Oxford Studies in Epistemology*, i. Oxford: Oxford University Press, 235–71.

Schaffer, Jonathan (2007). 'Knowing the Answer', *Philosophy and Phenomenological Research*, 75/2: 383–403.

Schaffer, Jonathan (2008). 'The Contrast-Sensitivity of Knowledge Ascriptions', *Social Epistemology*, 22/3: 235–45.

Schaffer, Jonathan (2012). 'Causal Contextualisms', in M. Blaauw (ed.), *Contrastivism in Philosophy*. London: Routledge, 35–63.

Schroeder, Mark (2007). *Slaves of the Passions*. Oxford: Oxford University Press.

Schroeder, Mark (2010). 'Value and the Right Kind of Reason', in R. Shafer-Landau (ed.), *Oxford Studies in Metaethics*, v. Oxford: Oxford University Press, 25–55.

Schroeder, Mark (2012a). 'Stakes, Withholding, and Pragmatic Encroachment on Knowledge', *Philosophical Studies*, 160/2: 265–85.

Schroeder, Mark (2012b). 'The Ubiquity of State-Given Reasons', *Ethics*, 122/3: 457–88.

Searle, John (2001). *Rationality in Action*. Cambridge, MA: MIT Press.

Sen, Amartya (1971). 'Choice Functions and Revealed Preference', *Review of Economic Studies*, 38/3: 307–17.

Sennet, Adam (2015). 'Ambiguity', in E. N. Zalta (ed.), *The Stanford Encyclopedia of Philosophy* (spring edn).

Sharadin, Nathaniel (2015). 'Problems for Pure Probabilism about Promotion (and a Disjunctive Alternative)', *Philosophical Studies* 172(5): 1371–86.

Sinnott-Armstrong, Walter (1992). 'An Argument for Consequentialism', *Philosophical Perspectives*, 6: 399–421.

Sinnott-Armstrong, Walter (2004). 'Classy Pyrrhonism', in Walter Sinnott-Armstrong (ed.), *Pyrrhonian Skepticism*. New York: Oxford University Press, 188–207.
Sinnott-Armstrong, Walter (2006). *Moral Skepticisms*. New York: Oxford University Press.
Sinnott-Armstrong, Walter (2008). 'A Contrastivist Manifesto', *Social Epistemology*, 22/3: 257–70.
Skorupski, John (2010). *The Domain of Reasons*. Oxford: Oxford University Press.
Skow, Bradford (2016). *Reasons Why*. Oxford: Oxford University Press.
Sloman, Aaron (1970). ' "Ought" and "Better" ', *Mind*, 79/315: 385–94.
Snedegar, Justin (2012). 'Contrastive Semantics for Deontic Modals', in M. Blaauw (ed.), *Contrastivism in Philosophy*. London: Routledge.
Stanley, Jason (2005). *Knowledge and Practical Interests*. Oxford: Oxford University Press.
Stanley, Jason (2011). *Know How*. Oxford: Oxford University Press.
Stratton-Lake, Philip (2005). 'How to Deal with Evil Demons: Comment on Rabinowicz and Rønnow-Rasmussen', *Ethics*, 115/4: 778–98.
Sturgeon, Scott (2010). 'Confidence and Coarse-Grained Attitudes', in Tamar Szabó Gendler and John Hawthorne (eds), *Oxford Studies in Epistemology*, iii. Oxford: Oxford University Press, 126–49.
Suikkanen, Jussi (2005). 'Reasons and Value: A Defence of the Buck-Passing Account', *Ethical Theory and Moral Practice*, 7/5: 513–35.
Suikkanen, Jussi (2009). 'Buck-Passing Accounts of Value', *Philosophy Compass*, 4/5: 768–79.
Temkin, Larry (1987). 'Intransitivity and the Mere Addition Paradox', *Philosophy and Public Affairs*, 16/2: 138–87.
Temkin, Larry (1996). 'A Continuum Argument for Intransitivity', *Philosophy and Public Affairs*, 25: 175–210.
Temkin, Larry (2012). *Rethinking the Good: Moral Ideals and the Nature of Practical Reasoning*. Oxford: Oxford University Press.
Temple, Dennis (1988). 'The Contrast Theory of Why-Questions', *Philosophy of Science*, 55/1: 141–51.
Toulmin, Stephen (1950). *Reason in Ethics*. Cambridge: Cambridge University Press.
Turri, John (2012). 'A Puzzle about Withholding', *Philosophical Quarterly*, 62/247: 355–64.
Väyrynen, Pekka (2010). 'A Wrong Turn to Reasons?' in M. S. Brady (ed.), *New Waves in Metaethics*. Basingstoke: Palgrave Macmillan, 185–207.
Way, Jonathan (2013). 'Value and Reasons to Favour', in R. Shafer-Landau (ed.), *Oxford Studies in Metaethics*, viii. Oxford: Oxford University Press, 27–49.

Wedgwood, Ralph (2009). 'Intrinsic Values and Reasons for Action', *Philosophical Issues*, 19: 342–63.
Williamson, Timothy (2000). *Knowledge and its Limits*. Oxford: Oxford University Press.
Yalcin, Seth (2011). 'Nonfactualism about Epistemic Modality', in A. Egan and B. Weatherson (eds), *Epistemic Modality*. Oxford: Oxford University Press, 295–332.

# Index

alternatives, sets of
  non-exhaustivity  6–7, 16, 34 n., 43, 59, 75, 77, 83, 128
  privileged  17, 62
  relations between  63–8, 82–8
  relevance  4–8, 13, 15–16, 32–6, 45–7, 65–8, 86–7 n., 108
  resolution sensitivity  6–7, 15–16, 75–6, 84–5
Alvarez, Maria  3 n.
Anderson, Elizabeth  30 n., 69

background conditions  55
Baron, Marcia  69 n.
Bedke, Matthew  69 n., 70 n.
Behrends, Jeff  70 n., 73, 74 n.
Blaauw, Martijn  3
Bratman, Michael  133
Broome, John  2, 14 n., 20, 30 n., 46 n., 64 n., 76 n., 80 n., 92 n., 94, 98

Cariani, Fabrizio  4, 5, 6, 15 n., 33, 50 n.
Chandler, Jake  3 n.
Chisholm, Roderick  123
Coates, D. Justin  70 n.
Comesaña, Juan  129
Condorcet  61, 127
Conee, Earl  123
contextualism  5, 7–8, 33–6, 47–9, 117 n., 133
contrastivism
  belief  3
  causation  3
  confirmation  3
  explanation  3, 8, 18–21
  justification  3, 8–13
  knowledge  3, 8, 10, 27
  metaphysical vs. semantic  5–6, 45–8
  'ought'  4, 8–9, 14–18, 48 n., 60–2, 78 n.
coordination across conjunction
  test  25–6
Crisp, Roger  29

Dancy, Jonathan  2 n., 3 n., 8 n., 14 n., 29, 51 n., 55, 66 n.
Danielsson, Sven  93 n.
D'Arms, Justin  117 n.
Darwall, Stephen  3 n.
deliberation  7, 14–16, 40, 55–6, 67–8, 87 n., 135, 136
Deliberative Constraint  55–6
DiPaolo, Joshua  70 n., 73, 74 n.
Dretske, Fred  3 n., 5 n., 6 n., 10, 11

Evers, Daan  72
evidence  11, 39, 117–18, 120–9
Exclusivity principle  29–31, 50–1

favoring
  contrastive  52–3, 58–9
  O-favoring  56–8
  and reasons  45–51, 58–9
Feldman, Richard  123
Finlay, Stephen  4 n., 5, 6 n., 20, 30 n., 33 n., 50 n., 68, 70 n., 72, 74 n., 76 n., 78 n.
Fitelson, Branden  3 n.
fitting attitudes  93
van Fraassen, Bas  3, 18 n.
Friedman, Alex  23, 64 n., 91 n., 92 n., 95, 98 n., 99 n., 100 n.
Friedman, Jane  116

Garfinkel, Alan  3 n., 18 n.
Glick, Ephraim  67 n.
Greenspan, Patricia  34 n., 80
Grice, H. P.  40
Groenendijk, Jeroen  4 n.

Hamblin, C. L.  4 n., 6
Hampton, Jean  21
Harman, Gilbert  130–1, 133, 135
Hieronymi, Pamela  2 n., 20 n., 118 n.
Higginbotham, James  4 n.
Hitchcock, Christopher  3 n., 18 n.

# INDEX

holism 8 n., 66 n.
Horty, John 14 n.
Hubin, Don 67 n.

intention
　coordinating role of 133–4
　reasons for 130–6
intonational stress 5, 33
intransitivty, *see* transitivity

Jackson, Frank 4 n., 14, 50 n., 73 n., 75
Jacobson, Daniel 117 n.

Karjalainen, Antii 3 n.
Kavka, Gregory 132
Kierland, Brian 4 n., 15 n.
Kolodny, Niko 69 n., 70 n.
Kratzer, Angelika 117 n.

Lehrer, Keith 38 n.
Lewis, David 6 n., 10
Lin, Eden 70 n.
Lipton, Peter 3 n., 18 n.

Mere Addition Paradox 100–1
Moore, G. E. 30 n., 68
Morton, Adam 3 n.

Nagel, Thomas 29, 30 n., 68, 77 n.
negative reason existentials 38–44
Nelson, Joe 56 n.
Norcross, Alastair 47–8
normativity 2, 20

objectives
　explanation of reasons 30–1, 56–8,
　　70–1, 81, 83, 87–8, 102–9
　importance of 103–9
　promotion of 31, 70–9, 81–2, 87–8
　what 68
Olson, Jonas 93 n., 118 n.
ought
　contrastivism about, *see*
　　contrastivism, 'ought'
　and reasons 2, 14–18, 21, 50, 59–62,
　　109–11, 115–18, 121–8, 130–7

Parfit, Derek 21, 30 n., 58, 68, 93–101, 111
Pargetter, Robert 73 n., 75
Paxson, Thomas 38 n.
Pettit, Philip 69 n., 139

Piller, Christian 118 n.
pragmatics 39–41
promotion
　in analysis of reasons 31, 68–82
　contrastive 74–82
　of desire, *see* objectives, promotion of
　probabilistic view of 70–1, 74 n.,
　　77 n., 78 n., 83 n., 85 n., 90
　of value, *see* objectives, promotion of

questions
　and contrastivism 4–7, 33, 133
　semantics of 4, 6–7, 33

Rabinowicz, Wlodek 93 n., 117 n.
Rachels, Stuart 23, 64 n., 91 n., 92,
　95, 96 n., 106 n.
'rather than' 1, 4, 7, 24–9, 32–8, 47, 52–7,
　81–2
rationality
　epistemic 114–19, 122–3, 131
　practical 114, 118, 129–36
Raz, Joseph 29, 46 n.
reasons
　analysis of 76–8
　circumstance-relativity of 7–8, 65–6
　epistemic 117–21
　explanatory 3, 18–21
　for and against 33–4, 77, 80
　instrumental 69
　moral 8, 47, 91, 96, 98–9
　motivating 3, 18
　normative 2–3, 9, 18–21, 46
　ontology of 2
　practical 117, 131–6
　*pro tanto* 2, 125 n.
　weight of 2, 15, 26–7, 40–3, 47–50,
　　61 n., 78, 81–2, 93, 103–12, 121, 124–7,
　　135–6
　wrong kind 117, 132
Reisner, Andrew 93 n.
Repugnant Conclusion 95–100, 107,
　109–10
Restricted Exclusivity principle 31–2,
　36 n., 52 n., 58, 74 n., 78, 81–2
Rickless, Samuel 27 n.
Roberts, Craige 5 n., 33
Rønnow-Rasmussen, Toni 93 n., 117 n.
Rooth, Mats 5 n.
Ross, Jacob 1 n., 52–3
Ruben, David-Hillel 27 n., 80 n.

Scanlon, T. M. 2 n., 21, 30 n., 45, 46 n., 58, 69, 93
Schaffer, Jonathan 3, 4, 5, 25, 26 n., 27 n.
Schroeder, Mark 3 n., 14 n., 16 n., 30 n., 31, 38–42, 46 n., 55, 68, 70 n., 72, 76 n., 77 n., 93 n., 117 n., 118–20, 123–4, 131 n.
Searle, John 20, 30 n., 76 n.
Sen, Amartya 84 n.
Sennet, Adam 25 n.
shallow contrastivism 22, 46–52, 63, 89
Sharadin, Nathaniel 70 n.
Sinnott-Armstrong, Walter 1 n., 3, 8–10, 13, 17–19, 24–7, 33 n., 80 n.
Skorupski, John 6 n.
Skow, Brad 18
Sloman, Aaron 4 n., 50 n.
Stanley, Jason 4 n., 119, 127
Stokhof, Martin 4 n.
Stratton-Lake, Philip 118 n.
Sturgeon, Scott 115 n.
Suikkanen, Jussi 93 n.

Temkin, Larry 23, 64 n., 91 n., 92 n., 94–102, 106 n., 108
Temple, Dennis 27 n.
ties 124–31, 135–6
Toulmin, Stephen 20, 30 n., 76 n.
transitivity
of 'better than' 92–4
of 'more reason than' 94–104, 106–13
of reasons 64–5, 82–3, 91–2, 101–7
Turri, John 129

undercutting defeat 39, 41

value
and reasons 30, 47, 68–9, 87–8, 93–4
promoting vs. respecting 31 n., 69, 87–8
Väyrynen, Pekka 46 n.

Way, Jonathan 93 n.
Wedgwood, Ralph 30 n., 68, 70 n.
Williamson, Timothy 119
withholding
as distinct attitude 115
reasons for 118–21, 124–9, 131, 133–6

Yalcin, Seth 6